YOU CHOOSE BOOKS™

THE WORLD WAR II SOLDIER'S EXPERIENCE

AN INTERACTIVE HISTORY ADVENTURE

CAPSTONE PRESS
a capstone imprint

You Choose Books are published by Capstone Press,
1710 Roe Crest Drive, North Mankato, Minnesota 56003
www.capstonepub.com

Library of Congress Cataloging-in-Publication Data
Cataloging-in-publication information is on file with the Library of Congress.
ISBN 978-1-4914-1713-3 (paper over board)
ISBN 978-1-4914-1514-6 (pbk.)

Photo Credits
akg-images: Ullstein bild, 122, 247; Alamy: Danita Delimont/Bernard Friel, 309, DIZ
Muenchen GmbH, Sueddeutsche Zeitung Photo, 59, 206, 241, Lordprice Collection,
234; AP Images, 183, U.S. Army, Wever, cover (top), 14; Bridgeman Art Library: Private
Collection/Charles Eddowes Turner, 139, SZ Photo, 128; Corbis, 227, Bettmann, 23,
24, 30, Hulton-Deutsch Collection, 258, 321, Sygma/John Van Hasselt, 288; Courtesy
of the Director, National Army Museum, London, 51; Courtesy of the National Park
Service, USS Arizona Memorial, 156, 163, 166, 176; Getty Images: Time Life Pictures/
William Vandivert, 257; Library of Congress, 283, 291, 316; MaritimeQuest: Michael W.
Pocock/Frank A. Stockwell, R.N. Collection, 319; NARA: U.S. Coast Guard/CPhoM.
Robert F. Sargent, 192, New Times Paris Bureau Collection/U.S. Information Agency,
230, U.S. Army photo, 38, 2d Lt. Jacob Harris, 107, Moore, 72, Spangle, cover (bottom),
102, U.S. Army Signal Corps Collection, 82, 86, U.S. Coast Guard Collection, 77, 198,
203, 214, U.S. Navy photo, 88, 187, 263, 275, 281, U.S. Office of War Information, 42;
Naval History & Heritage Command: U.S. Navy photo, 119, 210; Newscom: akg-images,
11, Mirrorpix, 135, 144; Rex USA: Associated Newspapers, 251; Shutterstock: Darren
Brode, 267; U.S. Air Force photo, 295, 301; USAFA McDermott Library SMA, 329, 307

Design Elements
Courtesy of Ingrid Dockter (dog tags); Shutterstock: Andrey_Kuzmin, aopsan, Nella,

Printed in Canada.
042014   008190FRF14

TABLE OF CONTENTS

WORLD WAR II

INFANTRYMEN:

AN INTERACTIVE HISTORY ADVENTURE

BY STEVEN OTFINOSKI

CONSULTANT:

DENNIS SHOWALTER, PHD

PROFESSOR OF HISTORY

COLORADO COLLEGE

TABLE OF CONTENTS

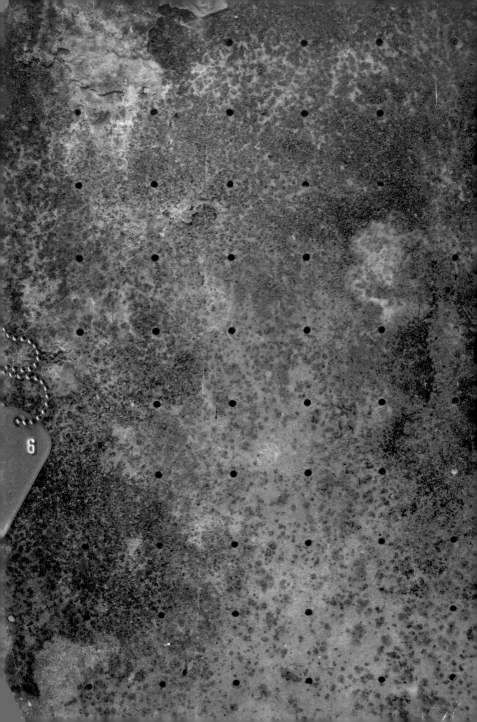

ABOUT YOUR ADVENTURE

YOU live in a world at war in the early 1940s. The Allies are fighting the Axis powers' attempt to take control of the world. What part will you play in the war?

In this book you'll explore how the choices people made meant the difference between life and death. The events you'll experience happened to real people.

Chapter One sets the scene. Then you choose which path to read. Follow the directions at the bottom of each page. The choices you make will change your outcome. After you finish one path, go back and read the others for new perspectives and more adventures.

YOU CHOOSE the path
you take through history.

WAR BEGINS

It is early 1942, and the world is at war. Germany, Japan, and Italy have joined forces. Together they have invaded country after country. These three nations are known as the Axis powers. The Allies will do all they can do to stop the Axis powers. The Allies are the United States, United Kingdom, Soviet Union, China, and those fighting with them.

The problems that started this war began more than 20 years ago. The first World War lasted from 1914 to 1918. It ended in defeat for Germany. The winners, including the United States, France, and Great Britain, dealt harshly with Germany.

9

Turn the page.

Germany lost all its colonies after the war. Its size was reduced by one-eighth. Its army and navy were also greatly reduced. The German economy declined and unemployment soared.

An economic depression in the 1930s also affected much of the world. People in some European nations looked to strong leaders to restore their nations' greatness.

Benito Mussolini came to power in Italy in the 1920s. By 1933 Adolf Hitler and his Nazi Party had control of Germany. Hitler's goals were to establish a German empire and get rid of people he called "undesirables." These people included the Jewish population of Europe. In May 1936 Italy and Germany signed a pact to work together.

Hitler (right) welcomed Mussolini to Germany in June 1940.

In 1938 Hitler began to put his plans into action. In March Germany took control of Austria. By October, it occupied neighboring Czechoslovakia. When Hitler invaded Poland on September 1, 1939, Great Britain and France declared war on Germany.

In April 1940 German troops occupied Denmark and attacked Norway. The next month Germany invaded Belgium and the Netherlands.

Turn the page.

By June 1940 France had fallen to the Germans. Italy invaded British African colonies in August and Greece in October. Japan invaded French territory in Asia in September. Meanwhile, Hitler set his sights on Great Britain. He launched an intensive air attack on the nation. But the British held out.

Frustrated, Hitler invaded Yugoslavia and joined Italy in attacking Greece in April 1941. Two months later he turned on the Soviet Union, launching a major attack on that vast nation.

Then on December 7, 1941, Japan launched a sneak attack on the American naval base at Pearl Harbor in Hawaii. The next day the United States declared war on Japan. Days later the United States declared war on Japan's allies, Germany and Italy.

Right now it feels like the whole world is fighting. The Allies are battling the Axis powers in three major parts of the world—the islands in the Pacific Ocean, North Africa, and Europe. You have joined the army and will fight for your country in the infantry. Where will you fight?

13

• To be an American infantryman in the Philippines, turn to page 15.

• To serve as a British soldier in North Africa, turn to page 43.

• To fight as an American soldier in the D-Day invasion in France, turn to page 73.

U.S. soldiers ducked for cover in a foxhole as the Japanese attacked on the Bataan Peninsula.

CHAPTER 2

HEAT IN THE JUNGLE

It is January 1942. Last month the Japanese began landing troops in the Philippines. Now Japanese forces have taken over nearly all of the island nation. American and Filipino soldiers have retreated to the Bataan Peninsula.

You are among the American infantrymen defending Bataan. General Douglas MacArthur is your commander. On February 22 President Franklin Roosevelt orders MacArthur and his staff to evacuate so the Japanese won't capture them. From Australia, MacArthur sends a statement to the Filipinos promising, "I shall return."

15

Turn the page.

General Jonathan Wainwright is now in command of the Allied forces in the Philippines. He is a good leader, but you wonder how long he can hold out against overwhelming odds. The Japanese have the Americans and Filipinos bottled up on the Bataan Peninsula.

The Japanese infantry is moving steadily forward. Food supplies are getting low on Bataan. Some of the men go into the jungle to hunt animals for food. They kill snakes, lizards, and monkeys. They even eat their own pack mules. The situation is growing desperate. It's only a matter of time before Bataan falls to the Japanese.

The island of Corregidor lies off the coast of Bataan. Wainwright is positioned on Corregidor, occupying an old Spanish fort called The Rock. He'll make his last stand there.

You could transfer to Corregidor before Bataan falls. There you could face a bloody battle, which you might not survive. But staying on Bataan and surrendering to the Japanese could bring an even worse fate. What will you do?

17

• To continue the fight on Corregidor, turn to page 18.

• To surrender to the Japanese at Bataan, turn to page 19.

You get your transfer to Corregidor. As the days pass, the Japanese step up their attack on the island. You and the other men flee to the long underground tunnel beneath the fort. Every time a shell lands on the fort, the ground shakes. Dirt and dust from the earthen ceiling fall on you.

On May 5 the Japanese come ashore on Corregidor and close in on the tunnel. General Wainwright fears there will be a last bloody battle. He urges the commanders still fighting outside the fort to surrender.

Many of your fellow soldiers are ready to surrender. But others plan to escape into the hills and continue fighting. You don't have much time to decide what to do.

• To flee to the hills, turn to page 27.

• To surrender, turn to page 38.

You surrender to the Japanese. You are one of more than 70,000 soldiers from Bataan who are now prisoners of war. The Japanese plan to march you 65 miles to the city of San Fernando. It quickly becomes clear that the Japanese will not be kind. They randomly beat you and the other prisoners.

You and two friends in your company, Frank and Tom, march in line with other prisoners. A truck pulls up on the dirt road. Inside sit rows and rows of Filipino prisoners. A Japanese guard climbs out of the truck's cab.

"We can take a few more," he says in English. Your friends shake their heads. These guards could be more cruel than the ones walking with you. But it is a long march to San Fernando.

• *To keep marching, turn to page 20.*

• *To get in the truck, turn to page 22.*

You decide against the truck, fearing what might happen if you leave the others. But you soon start to wonder if you made the right choice.

You march in rows of four. The hot sun beats down on you. You are tired from nights of little sleep and almost no food in the last days of the fighting. On top of that, the guards are cruel. One hits your head with the butt of his riffle.

You barely have the strength to lift your feet. Your body is bathed in sweat, and your throat burns with thirst. You ask one of the guards if you can have some water. He just smiles and dumps out a canteen of water on the ground in front of you.

You hear gunshots every now and then. But you are too focused on trying to walk to look at what or who is being shot. You can only think about water and rest.

Hours pass. It is late afternoon now, and it takes everything you have just to lift one foot after another. Finally you stumble on a root and fall.

"Get up," says Tom, holding out his hand and looking quickly over his shoulder.

You try to stand, but the ground feels soft and cool. Your body desperately needs rest. Lying here for just a few minutes would make you feel so much better. But will you be punished for falling behind?

• *To get up and continue marching, turn to page 24.*

• *To stay on the ground and rest, turn to page 40.*

You climb into the truck and wave good-bye to your friends. You promise yourself that you will find them later at San Fernando.

The ride is long and bumpy. But you're lucky. The guards driving this truck are kinder than others you've passed. Some other guards put a rope around a prisoner's neck and pulled him behind their truck. You push that image from your mind.

Late in the afternoon, the truck you're in gets stuck in the mud. The guards tell you and the others to get out and push. You all push hard, but the truck doesn't budge. The guards join you in pushing. You realize this might be the perfect time to escape into the jungle. But can you make it without getting caught?

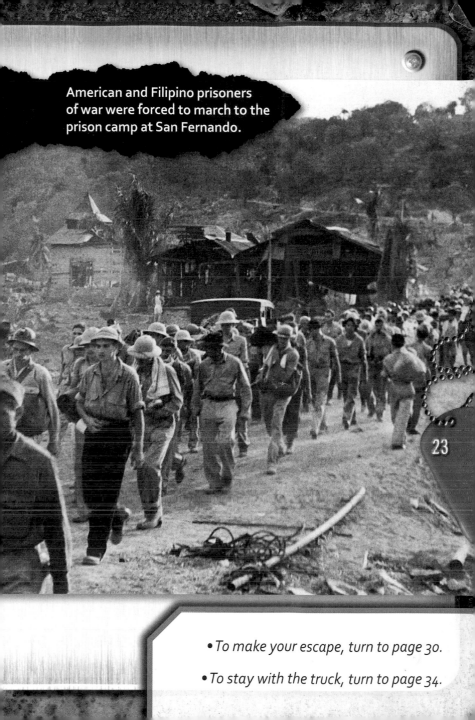

American and Filipino prisoners of war were forced to march to the prison camp at San Fernando.

23

• *To make your escape, turn to page 30.*

• *To stay with the truck, turn to page 34.*

You take your friend's hand and force yourself to your feet. He looks greatly relieved. You hear more gunshots in the distance.

"What is that?" you ask.

"It's the clean-up squad," explains Tom. "They're shooting those who fall behind. I saw them shoot a man who fell down earlier."

Guards stood watch over the prisoners, ready to use their rifles and bayonets.

24

You realize that shot could have been fired at you. Suddenly the march comes to a halt. A Japanese officer is speaking to the prisoners. He points to a nearby field.

"We will stay here for the night," he says.

Your captors wrap barbed wire around a group of trees. This will be your sleeping quarters. The Japanese herd you and the other prisoners behind the barbed wire like cattle.

You are given no food or water. You lie on the wet ground and listen to the moans of the men around you. Many of them are sick with malaria and dysentery. You vow that tomorrow you will escape this death march or die trying.

Turn the page.

In the morning you are awakened by a guard's rifle butt in your side. You line up with the other prisoners. You tell Frank and Tom about your plan to escape. You ask them to join you, but they shake their heads.

"It's too dangerous," says Frank. "You'll never make it."

"I've got to try," you tell them.

The march resumes. You are walking along a river. The bank is lined with tall grass. The guard in your outfit is distracted a few rows away. There may be no better time to make your move. But it's risky, and you may end up getting shot.

26

• *To attempt an escape, turn to page 28.*

• *To stay with the marchers, turn to page 29.*

You flee into the hills with other American soldiers before the surrender begins. The hills are steep, and soon you're panting in the heat. The jungle is so thick, and you're in such a rush to get away, that suddenly you're all alone. Where are your companions? A knot forms in the pit of your stomach. Maybe it was a mistake to escape.

It is getting late. The sun begins to sink. You have to decide what to do. Should you push on into the darkness to put more distance between you and the enemy? Or should you find a place to rest for the night?

• To keep going, turn to page 36.

• To rest for the night, turn to page 41.

The moment is right to make a break. You drop to the ground and roll away from the marching feet behind you. Other prisoners think you have fallen from fatigue and ignore you. As they pass, you roll into the tall grass along the riverbank.

You peer through the grass. Other groups of marchers are passing. Will one of the guards notice that you are missing from the line? You could dive into the river and cross to the other side, where you should be safer. Or is it better to wait until all the marchers have passed?

28

• To wait, turn to page 32.

• To dive into the river now, turn to page 37.

Your heart beats hard. You decide to wait. But as the day progresses, you find no better time to escape. The nearby guard has his eye on you. It's as if he knows what you're thinking.

One day blends into another. The guards are cruel. They beat and spit on the prisoners. They force you all to march in the hot sun with no rest. They give you no water or food. Your throat burns, and your thoughts spin. Some men are so desperate they dive for the dirty, muddy water on the side of the road. The guards shoot or stab anyone who steps out of the line.

After more than a week of this torture, you finally reach San Fernando. In all, only 54,000 of the 76,000 men who started the march finished it alive. And you are one of them. You have survived what will come to be called the Bataan Death March.

29

Turn to page 31.

You make your move. The guards are concentrating on the truck and don't see you sneaking into the jungle.

But the ground is muddy. The sucking sound of your boots in the mud attracts one guard's attention. He cries out. You run faster.

Suddenly two guards tackle you from behind. They tie you up with ropes and throw you on the floor of the truck.

After reaching San Fernando, prisoners were shipped in boxcars to Camp O'Donnell prison camp.

30

The San Fernando prison camp is a filthy place lined with barbed wire. You are jammed together with hundreds of other prisoners. Many of them are very sick. Guards toss the sickest men under the flooring of an old building, where they will soon die.

One evening the guards bring out large cans of rice. They begin to feed the men closest to the prison gates. You can almost taste the warm rice in your mouth. Then all at once, the guards take the cans away.

You are starving and exhausted. It feels as if you've been a prisoner for years, but it's only been a couple of weeks. But they have been the worst of your life. One morning you come down with malaria. You are soon burning with fever. When death nears, you look on it as a blessing. You will finally be free from this nightmare.

THE END

To follow another path, turn to page 13.
To read the conclusion, turn to page 103.

You decide to wait. You watch as the groups of marchers pass by. When they have all passed, you wade into the muddy waters of the river and swim across.

You climb out on the other side. Your clothes are soaked, but they dry quickly in the hot sun. The trail ahead leads deeper into the jungle. You were hoping to find friendly Filipinos who would help you. But you don't meet a soul.

As time passes you carve out a rough life for yourself. You make clothes from animal skins. You eat plants you find in the jungle and hunt animals with your bayonet. You even build a shelter not too far from Manila Bay. You think being close to the bay will give you the best chance of finding someone.

Every day you search for friendly Filipinos. One day you make your way to Manila Bay. You are shocked to find a band of Filipino guerrillas there.

"I've been living in the jungle since Bataan fell to the Japanese," you tell them.

"That was more than two years ago. It's 1944 now," one of the men tells you. You are stunned.

Then they give you the best news you've heard in a long time. "A few weeks ago, on October 20, MacArthur returned to the Philippines! He landed on the island of Leyte, southeast of here."

33

You breathe a sigh of relief. Soon MacArthur will lead the Allied forces to free the Philippines. You will finally be able to go home.

THE END

To follow another path, turn to page 13.
To read the conclusion, turn to page 103.

You decide not to risk an escape attempt. A few more minutes of pushing finally gets the truck out of the mud. You continue on your way.

In two days you arrive at the prison camp at San Fernando. It is a terrible place. You are locked in an area surrounded by barbed wire. In a few days the other prisoners begin to arrive on foot. Their eyes are hollow and their screams of pain and starvation never end. The guards crowd more than 1,000 other prisoners in with you. There are no bathrooms. Men have to relieve themselves right where they stand. Soon the smell becomes overwhelming.

Within the sea of faces, you see a soldier from your company. You shout to him and ask about your friends Tom and Frank. He pauses and swallows.

34

"They didn't make it," he says and turns away.

Your heart sinks. But maybe they're better off than being stuck in this filthy, horrible place.

Then one day the crowd starts moving. Guards force you and the other prisoners into boxcars. They shove more than 100 of you into a car that should only hold 25. Then they lock the doors. You have no idea where you're going or what might happen.

You think of your family back home and how much you miss them. You think of Tom's and Frank's families too. They don't know what's happened to their loved ones. You decide you must survive so that you can tell their families what happened. This alone will keep you going.

35

THE END
To follow another path, turn to page 13.
To read the conclusion, turn to page 103.

You decide to keep going. You'll put more space between you and the enemy, and it's cooler to travel by night. You step on grass that gives way under your weight. Suddenly you find yourself tumbling through space. You hit soft dirt and rise unsteadily to your feet. You have fallen into some kind of pit. Whether it was made by the Japanese or the Filipinos, you don't know. What you are sure of is that you are trapped.

You will sit and wait for morning, hoping that someone will rescue you. You pray that person is a friend and not an enemy.

THE END

To follow another path, turn to page 13.
To read the conclusion, turn to page 103.

You plunge into the river. The current is slow, and you swim with clean, confident strokes. You are in the middle of the river when you hear shots from the shore. Too late, you realize you should have waited. The guards heard the loud splash you made and have rushed to the riverbank. They are shooting at you.

The opposite shore is only a few yards away, but you will never make it there. You feel a sharp pain in your shoulder. Then a second bullet pierces your back. You sink below the muddy waters.

THE END
To follow another path, turn to page 13.
To read the conclusion, turn to page 103.

You and many other soldiers decide it's pointless to fight any longer. You ignore the whine of the falling shells and go to your underground barracks. You wash up, shave, and put on your best uniform. You will show the enemy that you are proud to be an American soldier.

As your captors lead you and the others out of the fort, you hear gunfire in the distance. Other soldiers outside the fort have ignored the order to surrender. They continue to fight the Japanese in foxholes.

Before the surrender, U.S. soldiers worked and lived in the underground tunnels at Corregidor.

The Japanese take you to a prison camp. You meet soldiers who surrendered at Bataan. A guy named John tells you hair-raising stories about the grueling 65-mile march they were forced to make.

"The Japanese soldiers beat us mercilessly. We couldn't even stop to use a bathroom."

"What happened if you tried?" you ask.

John drops his gaze. "They would kill you."

Camp life is harsh. Guards torture prisoners. Disease spreads like wildfire. So far you haven't caught anything. But you grow weak from the small rations of food. You cling to the hope that the Allies will win the war. If you're lucky, you'll still be alive to go home to your loved ones.

THE END

To follow another path, turn to page 13.
To read the conclusion, turn to page 103.

You stay on the ground. Your body is just too weak to go on right now. Tom tries to lift you, but he's as weak as you. He leaves you on the ground, whispering, "Good luck, friend."

After just a few minutes, you hear harsh voices speaking Japanese above you. You open your eyes. A Japanese officer and guard look down at you and smile.

Too late, you realize your mistake. The officer nods to the guard. The guard removes his pistol from its holster and aims it at your head. He fires twice.

40

THE END

To follow another path, turn to page 13.
To read the conclusion, turn to page 103.

You decide to rest. You lie down in a clearing and quickly fall asleep.

A bright light wakes you. An Asian soldier stands over you, pointing his rifle at your head. He asks in English who you are. You give him your name and rank. He lowers his rifle.

"My name is Emilio," he says. "I am a Filipino fighter. I'll take you to our camp."

Other soldiers who fled the fort are at this jungle hideout. You decide to join the guerrillas and fight the Japanese.

Life as a guerrilla isn't easy. Danger and death are always near. But you have hope one day the war will end, and the Philippines will once again be free. And on that day you will return home.

THE END

To follow another path, turn to page 13.
To read the conclusion, turn to page 103.

Bernard Montgomery (forefront) became one of the most famous generals of World War II.

SHOWDOWN IN THE DESERT

It is October 23, 1942. You are a British soldier in the 8th Army stationed in the Egyptian desert. Your commander is General Bernard Montgomery. You are stationed just outside the desert town of El Alamein, 60 miles west of the city of Alexandria. The Germans are dug in at El Alamein. The 8th Army's job is to drive them out.

The British have been fighting the Germans and their Italian allies in North Africa for two years now. German commander Field Marshal Erwin Rommel has again and again outsmarted previous British commanders. But Montgomery, or Monty as he is known to his troops, has a plan to beat him.

43

Turn the page.

Control of North Africa is important for both sides. If the Germans reach the Suez Canal in Egypt, they can control the flow of oil from the Middle East. The oil will fuel their tanks and other vehicles. Holding the Suez Canal will also give Germany control of North Africa and bring them closer to a final victory.

British Prime Minister Winston Churchill has been urging Monty for months to attack Rommel at El Alamein. But Monty won't be rushed. He spent all of September and most of October training new recruits. He has also trained you and other soldiers to defuse the thousands of land mines the Germans have scattered in the desert.

Monty also had his troops build dummy tanks, equipment, and soldiers in the south. He hopes these decoys will fool the Germans into thinking the attack will be there. But the real attack will be farther north.

Monty is ready for battle. The timing is good. Rommel is in Germany recovering from a stomach illness. The Germans won't have the "Desert Fox" to lead them.

The day of the attack is here. You know how to clear the mines. You also had some training in tank driving before you joined the infantry. But men to fight on the ground are needed too. How will you help?

• To work with the mine-clearing crew, turn to page 46.

• To drive a tank, turn to page 48.

• To march with the foot soldiers, turn to page 50.

Your job is to go ahead of the tanks and clear a path for them into El Alamein. The minefields stretch 5 miles across and 40 miles long. There are at least 500,000 mines buried here. Rommel calls it the "Devil's Gardens."

There is no way your crews can defuse all these mines. Your goal is to clear a path 24 feet across, big enough for two tanks to pass.

Your partner, Jim, pulls out his mine detector. When the electric coils in the detector pass over a metal mine, it's supposed to sound a signal.

Jim looks up from his detector. "It's not working," he says. Neither is yours.

This isn't surprising. Many of the detectors aren't working properly. Some soldiers use their bayonets to look for mines. They poke the long knives that are attached to their rifles into the ground. But you're not sure you want to do that. If you stabbed a mine, it could explode.

"We can get new detectors when the supply truck comes by," you tell Jim.

"We can't wait," he replies. "The tanks are coming, and we've got to clear a path for them."

• To use your bayonet, turn to page 53.

• To wait for new detectors, turn to page 66.

You approach the tank you'll be driving. It is a Sherman tank, one of 300 newly arrived from the United States. It's the best tank in the world. Its long-barreled guns can outshoot every Axis tank except the German Panzer IVs. And Rommel only has about 30 of those.

Your tank joins a hundred others lining up on the desert road to El Alamein. The tanks move at a snail's pace, following the marked path of the minesweepers. This is going to be a long night.

The flow of tanks slows to nearly a standstill. It is one huge traffic jam. The tanks must stay behind the minesweepers, and that is causing the tie-up.

Suddenly you hear a buzzing noise over the roar of the tank.

"What's that noise?" you ask.

One of your crewmates pokes his head out of the tank.

"German planes are everywhere!" he shouts. They're dropping bombs on the supply trucks."

Being stuck in this line makes your tank an easy target for the German artillery gunners. You don't have permission to leave the tank line. But if you stay where you are, you may be bombed at any moment.

49

• To cut out on your own, turn to page 54.

• To stay in line, turn to page 56.

You serve as a foot soldier. At 9:40 p.m. October 23, the order is given for the gunners to open fire on the German front. The sound of almost 900 artillery guns firing at once is deafening. Soon after the firing begins, Monty gives your unit the order to move forward.

You go before the tanks and most of the minesweepers. There is little danger of mines going off under your feet. It will take the weight of the tanks to set most of them off. That may be one reason why Monty has called this plan Operation Lightfoot.

You move forward through the smoke of battle. Within a few minutes, you're dodging bullets. You and your fellow soldiers drop to the sand. Up ahead you see the gunfire is coming from a foxhole. It is full of German soldiers.

You have two grenades in your pack. You could toss one of them at the foxhole. But the explosion may hurt Allied soldiers who are in the area. It might be better to get a little closer and fire on the foxhole with your rifle.

The smoke from the battle made it almost impossible for soldiers to see what was in front of them.

51

• To toss the grenade, turn to page 52.

• To get closer and shoot, turn to page 68.

You pull the pin and hurl the grenade at the foxhole. It explodes, and then the foxhole is silent.

Cautiously you move forward. Three soldiers lie dead in the foxhole. Several fellow infantrymen slap you on the back for a job well done. But you feel no satisfaction killing these men.

Then your radio crackles. "Retreat!" says a voice from headquarters. Operation Lightfoot has hit a snag. Soldiers around you start heading back to the start line. You feel numb about what you have just done. You need some time alone to think. But orders are orders.

- *To head back with the others, turn to page 58.*

- *To hang back for a few moments, turn to page 69.*

You decide not to waste time waiting for a new detector. You reach for your rifle and search for mines with your bayonet. You slice through the sand with the shiny blade. Jim does the same with his. Suddenly you strike something hard.

"I think I've found one," you say.

The two of you scrape away the sand. There is the mine. You begin to carefully remove the fuse. But the fuse is unfamiliar. You're not sure how best to remove it.

It might be better to leave the fuse as it is. But it could also be dangerous to move the mine with an intact fuse. Jim is just as unsure of what to do.

53

• To leave the fuse in the mine, turn to page 67.

• To try to defuse the mine, turn to page 71.

"Let's get out of here," you tell the other crew members.

"Right, mate," says Pete, the gunner. "We're just sitting ducks here."

You pull out of line and plow over the markers that show the safe road. You charge full speed ahead into the darkness.

You're almost to the front when suddenly you hit a mine. The tank is rocked by the explosion and stops dead in its tracks. Fire outside the tank quickly spreads inside. You throw open the hatch and leap out, your clothes aflame. You roll on the ground, putting out the fire.

You and your crewmates are all alive. But you've lost your tank. You're on foot in the midst of the battle.

Your first thought is to find another tank and hitch a ride. But your crewmate Steve doesn't agree.

"Better to hike it back to home base," Steve says. "We can get another tank there."

But you know it's unlikely you'll get another tank. Too many tanks have already been lost in this battle.

"There won't be room to ride in another tank," Steve reasons.

Your other crewmates side with Steve. But you still think getting on another tank might be safer than walking through a minefield.

55

• To try to hitch a ride, turn to page 57.

• To walk back to base, turn to page 70.

You take your chances and stay where you are in the unending line of tanks. You are lucky. The German artillery does not hit you or the other tanks in your caravan, although you have some close calls. Hours pass, and you make little progress. The cool desert night gives way to a blinding dawn.

Finally your radioman gets a signal. All tanks are recalled to base. You arrive safely back at base camp. You return to the barracks for some sleep and wonder what the next day will bring.

It is the morning of October 26. You learn that German General Georg Stumme, who is commanding while Rommel is sick, is missing. Later you hear that his car was hit by British gunfire, and he suffered a fatal heart attack.

56

Turn to page 58.

Hitching a ride on another tank is your best bet. At first you walk blindly in the desert darkness. Then the German bombs exploding overhead light the way to the tank caravan. Although they roll forward slowly, you're not sure they will see you. So you step dangerously close to the tanks' path. You pull off your shirt and wave it in the air to catch their attention.

But they don't see you in time. Before you can jump out of the way, you are hit by an oncoming tank. Unable to stop, the tank rolls over you, crushing every bone in your body. You are one of the first victims of the battle of El Alamein. And you're one of the few to be killed by your own side.

57

THE END
To follow another path, turn to page 13.
To read the conclusion, turn to page 103.

Rommel has been ordered back to the field from Germany to take command. Despite fighting hard, the Germans are in bad shape. They are low on fuel and supplies.

But Monty is taking no chances. In a few days he has come up with a new battle plan to drive the enemy out of El Alamein.

Monty reveals his new plan, called Operation Supercharge. Rommel is expecting you to attack again in the north. But Monty decides to surprise him with a major assault farther south. This time Monty will throw everything at the Germans at once—tanks, guns, and infantry.

You are eager to be a part of the action. Again, you have a choice. Both tank drivers and foot soldiers are needed.

Rommel (center) returned to El Alamein to find his troops losing the battle.

• To join the foot soldiers, turn to page 60.

• To command a tank, turn to page 63.

You have had enough of tanks. Your buddies in your infantry unit are glad to see you again. You begin the march into enemy territory. The minesweepers have done their work well, and you move quickly.

More than a week of bombing has left the Germans in bad shape. The farther you march, the more signs you see of defeat. Axis tanks and trucks litter the desert sands. There are bodies everywhere.

Suddenly, out of the smoke, you spy a group of four Germans on foot. They are carrying one of their wounded on a stretcher. It is your job to take them prisoner.

"Halt!" you cry out. But they only quicken their pace. "Halt or I'll shoot!" you cry again.

The retreating Germans are not stopping, despite your warning. You feel you have no choice but to fire. But can you do it?

61

• To shoot the Germans, turn to page 62.

• To hold your fire, turn to page 64.

You aim at the man in the rear of the group and shoot. He cries out and falls to his knees. The others put down the stretcher and open fire on you. You are hit twice in the leg and collapse to the ground. The Germans run away as your fellow soldiers surround you. Now you are the one who needs carrying.

By the time they get you back to the start line, you have lost a lot of blood. The British win the Battle of El Alamein, but you end up losing a leg.

THE END
To follow another path, turn to page 13.
To read the conclusion, turn to page 103.

You return to the tank division. Monty gives the order, and the tanks move forward. The Germans open fire. Many tanks around you burst into flames.

As the battle rages, a sandstorm hits. It offers protection from the enemy. The down side is that you can't see where you're going.

When the sandstorm finally dies down, you and your crew find yourselves in the open desert. You use maps and a compass to try to find the way back. Finally the gunner pokes his head out the hatch and yells, "Straight ahead! El Alamein!"

The town is in ruins. German forces have fled. You are disappointed to have missed the action but are grateful to be alive.

63

THE END
To follow another path, turn to page 13.
To read the conclusion, turn to page 103.

You can't bring yourself to fire. You watch the Germans disappear over the dunes. Perhaps they will be shot or captured by other British soldiers. But whatever happens, their blood won't be on your hands.

More tanks and trucks pass you on the road into El Alamein. Several of them stop and pick up you and your comrades. As you ride along, a jeep drives past at high speed. Sitting next to the driver is Monty. He is wearing a brightly colored scarf and waves at you and the others. There's a big grin on his face.

"Monty looks happy that we've won," says the driver of your truck.

"I bet Rommel isn't smiling right now," you say with a laugh.

In the days that follow, you realize how much this victory cost. Around 25,000 Germans and Italians have been killed or wounded. But at least 13,000 Allied troops were killed or wounded too.

You realize you're lucky to be alive. You hope your luck holds and the war ends soon.

THE END

To follow another path, turn to page 13.
To read the conclusion, turn to page 103.

You tell Jim you feel getting another detector is safer. He doesn't agree, but lets you have your way.

After a few minutes, the supply truck pulls up nearby. You begin to move toward it. "That's all right," says Jim. "I'll get it."

He heads toward the truck. BOOM! When the smoke clears, you see Jim lying on the ground, bathed in blood. He stepped on a small mine, the kind that can be tripped by a footstep.

Your friend is dead. It could have been you lying there. You will never forget this moment as long as you live.

THE END

To follow another path, turn to page 13.
To read the conclusion, turn to page 103.

66

You decide to leave the fuse alone. You don't want to accidently blow up the mine.

You carefully put the mine down on the ground. When the supply truck comes by, you can load it inside and have it brought back to base. There an expert can look at it.

As the supply truck comes rumbling toward you, a German shell whizzes down from the sky. It hits the mine, and the mine explodes. It kills you, Jim, and the driver of the truck. You never knew what hit you.

THE END
To follow another path, turn to page 13.
To read the conclusion, turn to page 103.

You crawl on your belly over the desert sand. A helmet peeks out of the foxhole. You stop and fire. The helmet disappears from sight. Did you hit the soldier under the helmet? You crawl closer to investigate. You feel a blazing pain as a bullet tears into your shoulder. You fire back. All is quiet in the foxhole.

You crawl closer and peer down into the foxhole. Below, a German soldier is lying still. Another is standing, clutching his side. You lock eyes, sharing a rare moment as two wounded soldiers, not as enemies. Soon British medics will bring help to both of you. For you and this German, the battle of El Alamein is over.

68

THE END
To follow another path, turn to page 13.
To read the conclusion, turn to page 103.

You don't want to be with the others, so you hang behind. You turn away from the soldiers you have killed, your mind filled with dark thoughts. Suddenly you feel a sharp pain in your side. You look down and see blood seeping from a wound. A soldier you thought you killed has just stabbed you with his bayonet. You turn your rifle on him and shoot. He slumps down, dead.

You are bleeding badly. You yell for help, but no one can hear you in the noise of battle. You suddenly feel very sleepy. In a few minutes, you fall into a sleep from which you will never wake.

69

THE END
To follow another path, turn to page 13.
To read the conclusion, turn to page 103.

It's a long and dangerous walk back to the base, but you make it safely before midnight. Lieutenant Jones, who sent you on this mission, is surprised to see you. You tell him what you did and what happened to your tank.

"Leaving the tank line was reckless and directly disobeying orders," he says. "You are a disgrace to your uniform."

Lieutenant Jones' words cut through you like a knife. You want to protest but can't find the words. You strike out with your fists instead. "Arrest that soldier!" cries the officer. You are hustled away and later court-martialed. You are sentenced to eight months in an Egyptian prison for striking an officer. The 8th Army goes on to win the battle of El Alamein, but you lose your freedom.

THE END
To follow another path, turn to page 13.
To read the conclusion, turn to page 103.

You can't leave the mine as it is. You have to defuse it.

Slowly you undo the fuse, bit by bit. Jim holds his breath as he watches you work. When the fuse is off and the mine is inactive, you both breathe a deep sigh of relief.

"That's another one down," Jim says.

You laugh at his remark. He grins back. This is just one mine out of hundreds that you and the other crews will disarm in the days to come. You are doing your part to clear a path for the tanks and foot soldiers to go forth into victory.

THE END

To follow another path, turn to page 13.
To read the conclusion, turn to page 103.

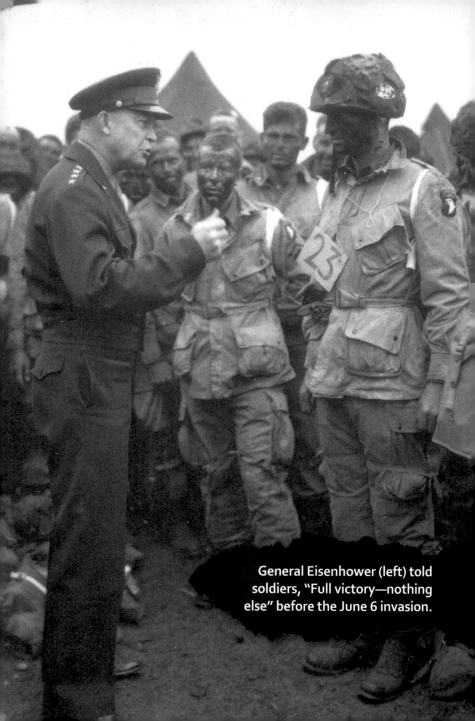

General Eisenhower (left) told soldiers, "Full victory—nothing else" before the June 6 invasion.

CHAPTER 4

INVASION AT NORMANDY

It is 4 a.m., June 6, 1944. You are on a ship in the English Channel between southern England and the northern coast of France. You are just one of about 130,000 soldiers waiting on the more than 5,000 ships.

You are part of the first wave of an Allied invasion to drive the Germans out of France. They have occupied France for four years.

Before you left England, American General Dwight Eisenhower addressed you and the other soldiers. "You are about to embark upon the Great Crusade," he said. Eisenhower is commander of the Allied forces in Europe and has been planning this invasion for months.

73

Turn the page.

The invasion was supposed to have taken place the day before. But bad weather caused a delay. Now as you look out at the choppy waters of the channel, you wonder how much the weather has improved.

Soon you and the other men move onto landing craft for the final leg of the trip. You will land on a beach in Normandy, France, code-named Omaha Beach. The boats are small. You feel the rolling waves much more than you did on the larger ship. Around you men are vomiting into little paper bags. You are feeling slightly sick yourself.

A strange silence falls over the boat as the shore comes into sight. You are about a quarter mile from land.

What awaits you on shore? Allied planes have been bombing the coast for weeks to drive the Germans back from the beaches. Maybe there will be no enemy waiting for you when you land. But that might be wishful thinking.

The shore looms closer. Men are getting nervous. Some are ready to jump into the water and wade to shore. Some of the men say if you wait until the beach to get off, you will be sitting ducks for German gunners on shore. Maybe they're right. You watch several soldiers leap into the water. Should you join them?

• To wait to get off, turn to page 76.

• To get off now, turn to page 78.

You'll stay on the landing craft until it gets closer to shore. You see many of the men who jumped off struggle in the deep water. You're glad you waited.

But as you get closer to the beach, you see German gunners firing. The coxswain in charge of the boat turns pale.

"You better get off now," he says to you and the other soldiers still on board.

"We can't," you reply. "We're still too far from shore. You need to get closer."

"I'm not going to risk my life," he says. "Get off. I'm turning this boat around."

The coxswain is endangering all your lives. But there's no time to argue with him.

You move to take control of the boat from the coxswain. He pushes you away. You come back at him and slug him in the stomach. He crumples to the deck. Six soldiers pin him down.

It's up to you now to bring the boat close enough to the beach so you and the other soldiers can get off. The only trouble is that you've never driven a boat before.

Tension was high for the troops on landing craft before the Normandy invasion.

Turn to page 82.

You put down your pack and rifle before entering the water. The deep water washes over your head.

Some of the men who got off can't swim. They splash helplessly in the water. One man seems to be drowning. You're a good swimmer and could possibly save him. But if you do, you will expose yourself to more German gunfire from shore.

- To swim to shore now, go to page 79.

- To help the drowning soldier, turn to page 80.

You decide not to help the drowning soldier. You feel bad about it, but you've got to think of your own safety. You swim toward shore with strong, swift strokes.

Suddenly water splashes wildly around you. The Germans are shooting at you from the beach!

If you dive underwater you'll be less of a target. But how long can you hold your breath? When you come up for air, you'll still be a target. Maybe it's better to keep your head above water so you can see what's coming.

79

• *To keep your head above water, turn to page 85.*

• *To swim underwater, turn to page 86.*

You swim to the drowning soldier. In his panic, he grabs you around the neck.

"Take it easy, or you'll drown us both!" you shout.

Your words calm him, and he loosens his grip. You wrap one arm around his shivering body and swim with your other arm. Slowly you move through the choppy waves.

The Germans on the beach have opened fire, but you manage to make it to land safely with your waterlogged friend. He has recovered and rushes up the sand behind you.

German soldiers are lined up along the plateau that looks over Omaha Beach. They fire machine guns, rifles, and bigger artillery at the soldiers below—at you. Everywhere you look there is confusion, smoke, and blood.

Soldiers who arrived ahead of you are struggling to get out of the line of fire. They are scrambling up the steep bluffs below the plateau. Then you notice a tank headed up the beach. Maybe you could run beside the tank for cover. But climbing to the plateau would get you off this dangerous beach.

81

• To climb to the plateau, turn to page 84.

• To hide by the tank, turn to page 87.

You gun the landing craft's engine. It leaps forward and speeds up the beach, coming to a sudden stop in the sand. You and the soldiers rush off, with the coxswain scrambling after you.

There are no other beached landing craft in the area. But there are plenty of other abandoned vehicles—tanks, transport ships, and supply units. But it's the bodies that make you stop. There are lots of soldiers, some dead, others wounded or dying, scattered along the beach. You are stunned, too dazed to move. Bullets zing all around you.

More than 34,000 U.S. troops landed on Omaha Beach on June 6, 1944.

Suddenly an officer runs up to you and the other men. You recognize him from the ship. He is Colonel George Taylor.

"Listen to me, men," he shouts above the noise of battle. "Two kinds of people are staying on the beach, the dead and those who are going to die. Now let's get the heck out of here!"

You get the message and follow Colonel Taylor up the beach to higher ground. You scramble up a steep bluff to the plateau above. You are lucky. There are no Germans there.

Some soldiers head the direction of a nearby village. Others are going out into the countryside. Either way, you're likely to meet more Germans.

• To enter the French village, turn to page 95.

• To go into the countryside, turn to page 97.

You follow other soldiers up toward the plateau. The bluffs look difficult to climb, but you have no choice if you are going to get off the beach. In all the smoke and confusion, you get separated from the other soldiers as you climb.

Suddenly you hear low voices speaking in German. You have stumbled upon an enemy machine gun nest. They are picking off the Americans landing on the beach. You think you can skirt around them and continue up toward the plateau. But if you can take out the German nest, you could save many lives below.

• To continue to the plateau, turn to page 92.

• To attack the machine gun nest, turn to page 94.

You keep swimming with your head up. You're almost to shore when you feel a sharp pang in your shoulder. You've been hit. Another bullet strikes your leg. You struggle to keep your head above water, but the pain of your wounds is too much. As you watch the boats draw close to the beach, you sink to the bottom of the sea like a stone.

THE END
To follow another path, turn to page 13.
To read the conclusion, turn to page 103.

You think it'll be safer to stay underwater. You take a deep breath and dive. You move quickly through the murky water. When you finally come up for air, you are almost on the beach. You wade to shore. The scene that greets you is a shocking one. Men are dying all around you. The water is stained red with their blood.

The high bluffs and steep cliffs made movement along Omaha Beach difficult even after the invasion.

As you race along the beach, you hear the roar of machinery. A tank is headed up the beach. You run alongside the tank, hoping it will offer some protection from the flying bullets.

The tank rolls up the beach. But suddenly the tread slips off, and the tank comes to a halt. The crew climbs out of the disabled tank. They head for the bluffs ahead and the plateau above them.

At either end of the beach are cliffs towering more than 100 feet. Some soldiers head for the cliffs, even though they appear far more difficult to climb than the bluffs. But German soldiers are firing from atop the bluffs. The cliffs, although a steeper climb, might not have Germans waiting to shoot you.

• *To climb the cliffs, turn to page 88.*

• *To climb the bluffs, turn to page 90.*

The cliffs are rocky, wet, and slippery. It's hard to get a grip as you climb. At times you feel yourself starting to slip, but you manage to hold on and keep going. A friend from your unit, Mike, is beside you. The two of you continue to slowly struggle up the cliff face.

Soldiers climbed the steep cliffs using only their hands or tiny rope ladders.

As you climb, Mike turns to you with a worried look on his sweaty face.

"I don't think I can make it," he gasps.

"We're almost there," you tell him. "You just have to hold on a little longer."

The top of the cliff is almost within reach when you hear Mike cry, "Help! I'm slipping!"

You turn to see his panic-filled face.

"Grab my hand," you tell him.

Mike puts out his hand. You lean down to grab it, but as you do, he falls. You watch in horror as he tumbles downward. Mike's final scream echoes in your ears—and it will for the rest of your life.

THE END

To follow another path, turn to page 13.
To read the conclusion, turn to page 103.

The path up the bluff is blocked with barbed wire and rocks that you and the other soldiers carefully walk around. You're worried the Germans have planted mines on the bluff, but you find none.

The top of the bluff is in sight. In a few moments you will be on the plateau. You pray that you will face no Germans there.

Your prayers go unanswered. A unit of German soldiers with rifles awaits you. They open fire. You leap into the air, and a bullet strikes your leg. Other men fall around you. Some of them are clearly dead. You are only wounded. But you lie still, hoping the Germans will take you for dead too.

They have no time to make sure you're dead. Their leader is barking orders. You open one eye and see them retreat from the advancing Allied forces. You continue to play dead until they are out of sight. Then you get up and look at the dead soldiers that surround you. You are bleeding and unable to walk. Soon the medics come and bandage your wound. You realize you're lucky to be alive.

THE END
To follow another path, turn to page 13.
To read the conclusion, turn to page 103.

You decide taking on the Germans alone is too risky. You quietly sneak around them, looking for a better place to continue climbing the bluff. But the bluffs are crawling with Germans. You can't find a clear path.

High cliffs tower over both ends of the beach. You head toward the cliffs. Some of the men from your unit are here, starting the dangerous upward climb on these 100-foot cliffs. Among them is your best friend, Ray.

"Be careful," Ray says when you arrive at the foot of the cliffs. "One misstep and you could fall and break your neck."

"Well, that's a better way to go than at the end of a German gun," you reply.

You both laugh, relieving the tension you feel. Then you begin to climb.

The top of the cliff is almost within reach when your hands begin to slip on the rocks. "Help!" you cry. Ray puts out his hand. Your hands are sweaty, but somehow you manage to hold onto your friend. Finally you get your grip on the rock again. You take a quick look down and breathe a sign of relief. The rocks below almost became your grave.

THE END

To follow another path, turn to page 13.
To read the conclusion, turn to page 103.

You reach into your pack and lift out one of four grenades you have been issued. In your nervousness, you drop the grenade. It starts to roll down the sandy slope. You run to retrieve it.

You pick up the grenade and pull the pin. But you wait a moment too long to hurl it at the Germans. It explodes in your hand.

The explosion blows away your hand and part of your arm. You lie bleeding on the ground. The Germans in the gun nest hear the explosion. They aim their machines guns at you and quickly put you out of your misery.

94

THE END
To follow another path, turn to page 13.
To read the conclusion, turn to page 103.

You join the other soldiers heading for the village. It is only a few miles away. When you reach it, the village is strangely quiet.

"The villagers must have fled when the Germans started bombing," says a soldier.

You walk down a street and see other American soldiers preparing to leave the village.

"We have orders to go to the town of St. Lo," one soldier tells you. "The Germans are holed up there. It should be some battle."

You're not ready to fight another battle. It'd be nice to stay here in the village for a while. But you may be needed to fight the Germans in St. Lo.

• To rest in the village, turn to page 96.

• To join the soldiers headed for St. Lo, turn to page 100.

You need a rest. You and some other soldiers find a deserted shop and fill up on fresh bread and cheese. Then you walk into a nearby field. The field is green, and the air you breathe is fresh and clean.

As you walk, you see an elderly Frenchman across the field waving wildly at you. You wave back. Now he is crying out to you in English. "Watch out!" he cries. "Mines!"

You stop in your tracks, but not soon enough. The field is loaded with small German mines that are easily triggered by a man's weight. You step on one and it explodes, killing you instantly.

96

THE END
To follow another path, turn to page 13.
To read the conclusion, turn to page 103.

You head out for the countryside. A few miles down the road, you come to a stone farmhouse. A woman rushes out the door.

"American?" she says in a French accent.

"*Oui*," you say. It is one of the few French words you know.

She hugs you and speaks rapidly in French. Her name is Emilie. She takes you inside and introduces you to her husband, Henri.

As Emilie prepares you a meal, there is a knock at the door. A harsh voice says something in German.

The couple motions for you to hide in their bedroom. But your first instinct is to run out the back door.

• To hide in the house, turn to page 98.

• To escape out the back, turn to page 101.

You follow Henri into the bedroom. He pulls clothes from a dresser. You change and shove your uniform into a drawer. Just then the door opens, and a German officer enters. He asks you something in French. You say nothing and pretend to be putting clothes away.

Emilie comes to your rescue. She points to her ear as she jabbers in French. She is telling the officer that you are deaf.

The German stares at you for a long time. Then he seems to accept her story and leaves. You breathe a sigh of relief.

As soon as the officer and his men have left, Emilie gives you some food wrapped in a cloth. Then the couple sends you on your way. You will never forget their kindness.

The Germans are in full retreat from Normandy now. You link up with your unit and continue to advance south. On August 25, 1944, you enter the French capital of Paris. The Germans have fled.

The people of Paris celebrate your arrival. There is music and dancing in the streets. It seems a lifetime ago since you landed on Omaha Beach. The invasion that so many soldiers gave their lives for has succeeded. The Germans have lost nearly all the territory they held for four years. It can't be long before the war is over.

99

THE END
To follow another path, turn to page 13.
To read the conclusion, turn to page 103.

You join the soldiers marching to St. Lo to fight the Germans. It is a long trip. St. Lo is not far, but the Germans are everywhere. They fight your advance through the countryside. You spend weeks in a soggy field, waiting for more Allied troops to join you. On July 11 you close in on St. Lo, and the battle begins.

The fighting is fierce, but the town falls to the Allies in about a week. The Germans retreat. Much of St. Lo has been reduced to rubble, but victory is yours.

You are transferred to the 4th Division, which is marching farther northeast toward the capital city of Paris. You arrive there in about six weeks. The Germans have fled. Paris is free. You hope the end of the war is near. You can't wait to go home.

THE END
To follow another path, turn to page 13.
To read the conclusion, turn to page 103.

You are afraid of being caught in the house. You rush out the back door. Angry voices call to you in German. You run faster. You hear shots and feel a stab of pain in your side. You stumble and fall.

In moments, two German soldiers with rifles are standing over you. They are quickly joined by their officer. He barks a command and the two soldiers lift you to your feet. Other soldiers return to the farmhouse. You hear shots and cries. Emilie and Henri have paid for their kindness with their lives.

The Germans will be moving out to keep ahead of the invading Americans. And you will go with them as a prisoner of war.

THE END
To follow another path, turn to page 13.
To read the conclusion, turn to page 103.

Infantrymen used tanks for cover as they marched into towns.

CHAPTER 5

THE WAR ENDS AT LAST

World War II lasted more than six years. Eventually the Allies pushed the Axis powers out of the countries they had invaded. The infantrymen who battled on the ground were a main reason the Allies won the war.

The infantry made great sacrifices, fighting and dying in one major battle after another. Infantrymen were killed and wounded. Others were captured and held as prisoners of war. Still others went missing in action. Of the U.S. Army casualties in the war, about 80 percent were suffered by the infantry. The 3rd Infantry Division alone reported nearly 26,000 casualties.

Infantrymen were sent into battle again and again during the war. The average foot soldier faced 45 days of combat, but some units and divisions were under fire for longer. The 32nd Infantry Division, which served in the Pacific, was in combat for 654 days. In combat or out of it, infantrymen were away from their homes and loved ones for a long time.

For many, gunfire wasn't the only threat to their health. Many infantrymen fought in extreme conditions—the hot, burning sands of North Africa or the steamy, humid jungles of the Pacific islands. Others suffered frigid cold in parts of Europe.

The infantry's sacrifices helped the Allies to victory over the Axis powers. The British Army's powerful assault of foot soldiers and tanks on El Alamein, Egypt, drove the Germans out of Egypt. That battle effectively ended the Germans' hopes of conquering North Africa.

American and Filipino soldiers weren't able to stop the Japanese from taking the Philippines. But they showed great courage on the Bataan Death March and in the terrible Japanese prison camps. News of cruelties committed in these places made the Allies more determined than ever to defeat the Axis powers.

The massive invasion of Normandy on D-Day soon drove the Germans out of France. This victory paved the way to the end of the war.

The infantry's strength and courage were demonstrated in hundreds of other battles throughout the war. British infantry landed in Sicily off the coast of Italy in July 1943 and took the entire island in just 39 days. During this time Mussolini fell from power, and the Italians surrendered to the Allies.

Allied infantry faced stiff resistance in the Battle of the Bulge. In the Ardennes Forest of Belgium and France, the Germans made a last stand in December 1944. The Allies were driven back by 38 German divisions, until British armored units broke through the enemy lines from the south. By January 1945 the U.S. infantry had recovered every bit of land lost to the Germans.

U.S. infantrymen looked for any hidden enemies in Waldenburg, Germany, near the end of the war.

The infantry's efforts freed millions of people worldwide. It took years for war-torn nations to recover. But without the infantry and its sacrifices, that recovery might never have happened. Men on foot, armed with only a few weapons and brave hearts, won the war and changed the world.

TIMELINE

1922—Benito Mussolini becomes prime minister of Italy.

1933—Adolf Hitler comes to power in Germany.

May 1939—Hitler and Mussolini sign the "Pact of Steel," a pact for world domination.

September 1, 1939—Germany invades Poland. Two days later Great Britain and France declare war on Germany, setting off World War II.

June 22, 1940—France falls to Germany, following several other Western European nations.

December 7, 1941—The Japanese launch a sneak attack on the U.S. naval base at Pearl Harbor, Hawaii.

December 8, 1941—The United States declares war on Japan.

February 22, 1942—U.S. General Douglas MacArthur withdraws from the Philippines.

April 1942—Thousands of American and Filipino soldiers surrender to the Japanese on the Bataan Peninsula.

May 1942—The Battle of Corregidor ends in a Japanese victory; about 650 American prisoners of war die on the Bataan Death March.

October 23, 1942—The battle of El Alamein begins, pitting the British against the Germans in the Egyptian desert.

November 1, 1942—General Bernard Montgomery launches the final phase of the battle, Operation Supercharge; within days the Germans under Field Marshal Erwin Rommel are in retreat.

June 6, 1944—The Allies launch a massive invasion of the Normandy coast of German-occupied France.

August 25, 1944—The Allies free Paris.

December 1944–January 1945—Germany makes a last stand in Belgium at the Battle of the Bulge.

April 30, 1945—Hitler commits suicide in his bunker in Berlin, Germany; Germany surrenders a week later.

August 6–9, 1945—American planes drop atomic bombs on the Japanese cities of Hiroshima and Nagasaki.

September 2, 1945—Japan officially surrenders, bringing World War II to an end.

OTHER PATHS
TO EXPLORE

In this book you've seen how the events experienced by World War II infantrymen look different from three points of view.

Perspectives on history are as varied as the people who lived it. You can explore other paths on your own to learn more about what happened. Seeing history from many points of view is an important part of understanding it.

Here are some ideas for other World War II points of view to explore:

+ Filipinos fought side by side with Americans in the Philippines. But unlike their allies, they were fighting for their homeland. How was their war experience different?

+ During the war German leader Adolf Hitler had millions of European Jews killed. What was the war like for these people?

+ American women were not allowed to be soldiers in World War II. But many of them served their country in other ways, both at home and abroad. What was their war experience like?

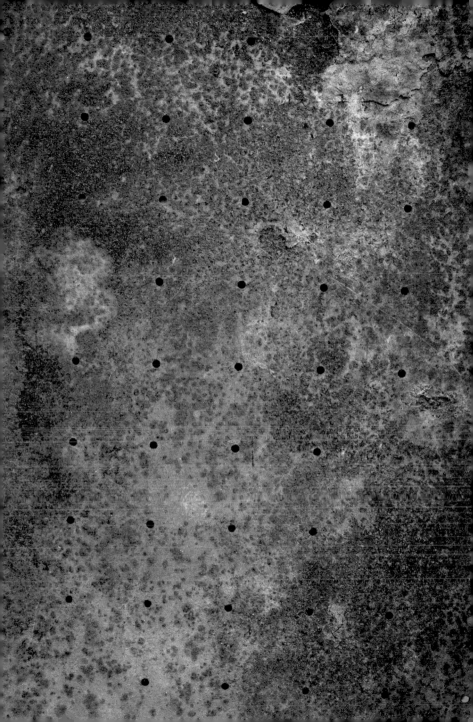

WORLD WAR II
NAVAL FORCES:

AN INTERACTIVE HISTORY ADVENTURE

BY ELIZABETH RAUM

CONSULTANT:
DENNIS SHOWALTER, PHD
PROFESSOR OF HISTORY
COLORADO COLLEGE

TABLE OF CONTENTS

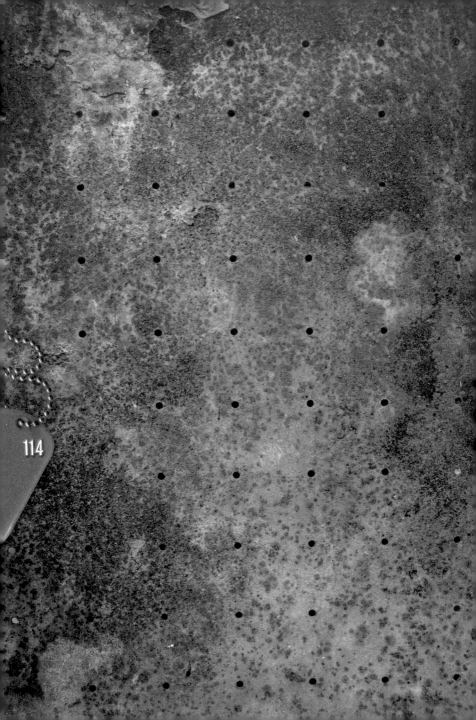

ABOUT YOUR ADVENTURE

YOU are living in a world on the brink of war. The Second World War is about to begin. Will you join in?

In this book you'll explore how the choices people made meant the difference between life and death. The events you'll experience happened to real people.

Chapter One sets the scene. Then you choose which path to read. Follow the directions at the bottom of each page. The choices you make will change your outcome. After you finish your path, go back and read the others for new perspectives and more adventures.

YOU CHOOSE the path
you take through history.

EUROPE

| ALLIED CONTROLLED | AXIS CONTROLLED | NEUTRAL NATIONS |

ASIA

WORLD WAR II,
ALLIED AND AXIS TERRITORIES
IN EUROPE AND ASIA

JOINING THE NAVY

Dad shakes his head as he puts the newspaper down. "I'm afraid we're headed for war again," he says. "Your uncle died on a battlefield in France in 1917. That war was supposed to be the 'war to end all wars.'"

"What makes you think there will be another?" you ask.

"The paper reports that Adolf Hitler just passed a law requiring all German men to serve in the army. He must be planning for war."

"With luck, any fighting will be over by the time you turn 18," Mother says.

"That's years from now," you say. But you think that fighting a war sounds exciting.

Turn the page.

You begin following the news in the papers, just like your dad does. Germany is not alone in preparing for war. In 1936 Italy and Japan join with Germany to form the Axis powers. Italy, under its dictator, Benito Mussolini, wages war in Africa. In Asia, Japan is invading China.

In 1938 you read about the German Army's march into Austria. The next September you hear that 1.5 million German troops attacked Poland and claimed that nation for Germany.

Britain and France declare war on Germany. They call themselves the Allies. Australia, New Zealand, Canada, India, and South Africa join the Allies. Later the United States and the Soviet Union will become Allies too.

Sailors on the USS *Ward*, a destroyer, fired the first American shot in the battle that led the United States to enter WWII.

After the defeat of Austria and Poland, German troops invade Belgium, Norway, France, and the Netherlands. France falls to the Germans on June 22, 1940. Then Hitler turns his attention toward Great Britain.

By now you're old enough to think about enlisting in the military. Dad and Mother worry, but you've already decided that you'll join a naval force. The sea has always fascinated you. Imagine seeing the world from the deck of a huge ship!

Turn the page.

You read about the world's navies. Great Britain is already using its navy to protect merchant ships bringing supplies from North America to Europe. The advancing German Army has cut off supplies from Europe. Much of Great Britain's food, medical supplies, and military supplies are now shipped from Canada and the United States. Keeping the shipping lanes open across the Atlantic Ocean is necessary for Great Britain's survival.

Shutting down that supply route is Germany's goal. Germany uses submarines called U-boats to attack the merchant ships. In the first few months of 1940, German U-boats sank 110 merchant ships. Germany is also building large battleships.

Meanwhile, the U.S. Pacific fleet remains anchored in Pearl Harbor, Hawaii. So far the United States is not involved in the war.

The world's navies will play a major role in the war. Whether they serve on battleships, submarines, or landing crafts, navy members will be in the middle of the action.

• To serve as a sailor on the German battleship Bismarck, turn to page 123.

• To experience the Japanese attack on Pearl Harbor as a U.S. Marine, turn to page 151.

• To serve in the U.S. Navy during the D-Day invasion, turn to page 183.

The battleship *Bismarck* (below) and its sister ship, *Tirpitz*, were the biggest battleships Germany ever built.

CHAPTER 2

SINK THE *BISMARCK*!

Soon after you turn 18, you and your friend
Hans join the Kriegsmarine, Germany's navy.
After basic training you're assigned to the
Bismarck, the biggest battleship in the world.
It's bigger than the HMS *Hood*, Great Britain's
most famous World War I battleship.

"The *Bismarck* is newer and more powerful,"
you tell Hans. "If the *Bismarck* ever battles the
Hood, the *Bismarck* will win."

Hans smiles. "Of course!"

The *Bismarck* will be home to more than
2,000 men. They will need cooks, barbers, tailors,
and doctors, as well as deckhands. You happen to
mention that your father is a barber.

123

Turn the page.

"The ship needs a good barber," your commanding officer says. But Hans wants you to be a deckhand like him.

You'd get to spend your days outdoors as a deckhand. But being a barber might give you a chance to interact with the officers.

- *To serve as a deckhand, go to page 125.*

- *To serve as a barber, turn to page 127.*

You choose to work on deck. You report to the dock in Gdynia, Poland, in early April 1941. The *Bismarck* looms before you like a great gray whale. The ship is more than 800 feet long. Steel armor covers every visible surface. It looks indestructible.

Lieutenant Engel gives you your assignments. You'll scrub the decks and maintain the life rafts. And you'll handle the lines that connect the ship to the dock.

The ship has four big gun turrets. Each one holds two 15-inch guns. They're the biggest guns ever mounted on a German battleship. You will assist the gunnery crew at one of the turrets.

"This is your battle station. Whenever the alarm sounds, you are to report to this turret immediately," Engel says sternly.

125

Turn the page.

On May 18 the *Bismarck* pulls away from the wharf. The *Prinz Eugen*, a smaller, faster ship, will escort you on the mission. After two days at sea, the *Bismarck*'s commander, Captain Ernst Lindemann, says, "We're heading to the Atlantic. Our goal is to sink ships carrying supplies to Great Britain." It's a secret mission—and an important one.

Now that you're in the North Sea, Captain Lindemann orders four-hour watches. You stay on deck for four hours, sleep for four, and then return to watch. After a day or two, you're exhausted. You are sleeping soundly when the alarm bells sound. Is it part of your dream?

- *To go to your battle station, turn to page 132.*
- *To ignore the alarm, turn to page 134.*

"My son, a navy barber!" Dad says proudly.

"And you'll be safe below deck," Mother adds.

The ship is huge, but space for sleeping, eating, and haircutting is tight. The *Bismarck* is made for battle, not convenience. You're assigned a battle station near one of the gun turrets. "We'll need every hand on deck during a battle," your commander says.

Many officers confide in you as you cut their hair. In early March 1941 one of them says, "Chancellor Hitler plans to visit. Imagine that—our great leader on board the *Bismarck*."

Deckhands scrub the decks, laundry workers press uniforms, and you work overtime making the officers look their best. You put on your dress uniform and line up with the crew.

Turn the page.

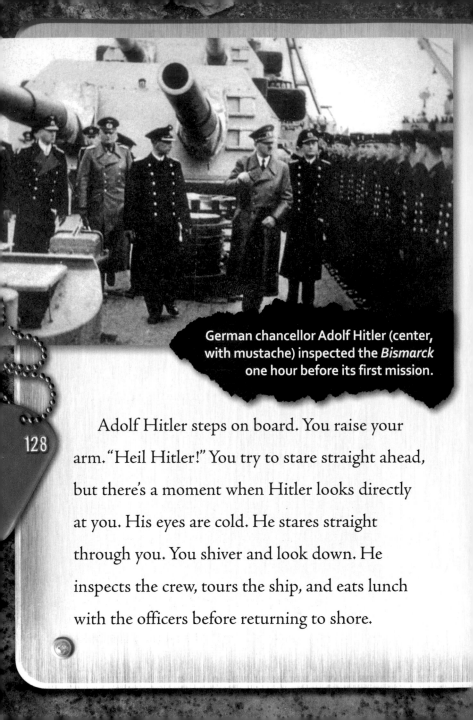

German chancellor Adolf Hitler (center, with mustache) inspected the *Bismarck* one hour before its first mission.

Adolf Hitler steps on board. You raise your arm. "Heil Hitler!" You try to stare straight ahead, but there's a moment when Hitler looks directly at you. His eyes are cold. He stares straight through you. You shiver and look down. He inspects the crew, tours the ship, and eats lunch with the officers before returning to shore.

On May 18 the *Bismarck* leaves dock. A few days later you notice that the big swastikas on the deck have been painted over. "We don't want enemy airplanes to know we are German," an officer explains. "We're going to the Atlantic to sink merchant ships carrying supplies from North America to Great Britain. Without supplies the British are sure to give up."

The ship's alarm sounds at 4:11 p.m. on May 23. You scramble up the ladder to your battle station. "False alarm," a sailor reports. The cold wind and heavy fog have put everyone on edge.

The alarm sounds again an hour later. You are cleaning the barbershop. An officer suggests you finish up. "It's probably another false alarm," he says.

• To report to your battle station, turn to page 130.

• To finish cleaning up, turn to page 136.

129

"I don't think it's a false alarm," you say. You race up the ladder toward your battle station. The deck is slippery with ocean spray. You are running too fast. You slide across the sea-soaked deck and slam into one of the big metal gun turrets. "My leg!" you shout before blacking out.

You awaken in the sick bay. A medic says, "You broke your leg. You've been unconscious for hours."

Hans stops by for a quick visit. "We sunk the *Hood*!" he tells you. "Now the British are after us. We're leaking oil and taking on water."

Hans hurries back to his battle station. The crew is on constant watch. No one has time to eat or sleep. The alarm sounds again and again, but you're stuck in bed.

The seas are rough. Seasick sailors report to the sick bay. They are sent back to their stations after a brief rest. Around noon a message comes over the loudspeakers:

"Seamen of the battleship *Bismarck*! We will fight until our gun barrels glow red-hot and the last shell has left the barrels. For us seamen, the question now is victory or death."

You drift to sleep and wake to a nightmare. Guns roar. The ship quakes. British bullets rain down on the metal deck above.

You want to help. When the ship rolls to the side, a closet door swings open. Medical supplies scatter. Several crutches land nearby.

131

• *To get out of bed, turn to page 141.*

• *To stay in bed, turn to page 142.*

You grab your life jacket and head for your battle station. Guns flash in the distance. "There's a ship heading our way, and it's firing!" a seaman shouts. The first salvo from the enemy splashes harmlessly into the ocean.

"The *Hood*—it's the *Hood*!" an officer shouts.

The gunnery commander waits until the ship is within firing range. Finally you hear the words "Permission to fire!" The roar is deafening. You put your hands up to cover your ears. Thick smoke chokes and blinds you.

"She's blowing up!" the officer shouts. Eight minutes into the battle, the *Hood* explodes and sinks. You and your mates cheer. You've sunk the mighty *Hood*!

However, the *Bismarck* has not escaped unharmed. Water is pouring in through a hole in the hull. Oil is leaking out. But the *Bismarck* speeds forward—other British ships may be chasing it.

Ever since the *Bismarck* reached the open waters of the Atlantic Ocean, Captain Lindemann has required the crew to be on constant watch. During one especially sleepy shift, your replacement shows up early. He offers to take over. You're hungry and so is the crew. Maybe you should go to the canteen for some food and bring something back to the others.

133

• *To finish your shift, turn to page 137.*

• *To go to the canteen, turn to page 148.*

Hans shakes you awake. "It's not a drill!" You throw on your clothes and climb topside to your battle station. Five minutes later, at 5:52 a.m., the British begin firing.

"It's the *Hood*!" an officer shouts. The enemy ship's guns are aimed at the *Bismarck*. But its first salvos fall short.

An officer shouts, "Permission to fire!" When the guns go off, it's like standing next to an exploding bomb. It's so noisy that your teeth rattle.

"She's blowing up!" Flames cover the *Hood*, and within seconds, she sinks.

You cheer. "We did it!" you yell. Then you realize that the British ship was filled with sailors just like you. "It could have been us," you say.

"But it wasn't," Hans replies.

HMS *Hood*, the Royal Navy's largest warship, was sunk during a battle with the *Bismarck*, killing more than 1,400 British sailors.

Captain Lindemann orders continuous watch. "The British are chasing us," Lieutenant Engel confides. Your four-hour watch is over. You are ready to drop with exhaustion. "Will someone go to the canteen to get food for the crew?" Engel asks. You need a nap more than food, but your crewmates do look hungry.

• To take a nap, turn to page 139.

• To go get food, turn to page 148.

You stay below to clean up. But this time the fight is real. It only lasts for 8 minutes. The crew of the *Bismarck* has blown the HMS *Hood* to bits. "We did it!" Hans yells. You cheer along with him.

"Our rudders have been damaged," Captain Lindemann says a few hours later. "We're going to France for repairs."

As you steam toward France, British planes buzz overhead. Guns boom constantly. A torpedo slams into the deck. Alarms sound on the morning of May 27. You report to your battle station. Strong winds whip around you. Rain pelts your face. "Two British ships," Hans says. "Maybe three. They want revenge."

"The ship is burning!" someone yells. "Save yourselves!" Some men are jumping overboard. Wait! Where did Hans go?

• To save yourself, turn to page 143.

• To find Hans, turn to page 147.

"I'll finish my shift," you tell your replacement. British torpedo planes buzz overhead. "Fire!" your commander orders. The planes fly away, but before long, they're back.

A torpedo slams into the starboard side of the deck, opposite your turret. The blast kills one seaman and damages the ship's boiler. Your hands shake and your heart thuds with each blast. No place is safe in war.

You fire and reload endlessly, losing track of time. Sometime later the admiral's voice comes over the loudspeaker. You only catch his final words: "For us seamen, the question now is victory or death." The words frighten you.

Turn the page.

You stay by the turret all night. Gunfire lights up the night sky. By the next day you're exhausted. Four hours of sleep is not enough. You're not the only one who falls asleep standing up.

Toward morning someone yells, "British ships!" The final battle has begun. "It's the *Rodney!*" a sailor yells. "And the *King George V,*" says another. Shells batter the *Bismarck*'s deck. A fire begins burning nearby. Soon the entire ship is on fire. "Abandon ship!" an officer orders.

You run to the battery deck where the guns are mounted. Men are tossing inflatable life rafts into the sea. "Jump!" a sailor yells. It's a long way down, and you're not a strong swimmer.

• To jump, turn to page 146.

• To look for a life jacket, turn to page 149.

You're too tired to eat. You hurry to your quarters and crawl into your hammock. You're barely asleep when the alarm bells begin ringing. There's a deafening blast. The ship shudders and seems to scream. You leap out of your hammock and throw on your life jacket. "We've been hit!" an officer yells. "Get out! Get out now! Follow me!"

British ships and aircraft pursued and attacked the *Bismarck*, avenging the loss of the *Hood*.

Turn the page.

He leads you to a narrow tube that goes topside—to the deck surface. "Climb!" he shouts.

You remove your life jacket to fit inside. You pull yourself up the ladder, climbing as quickly as you can toward the light at the top. Several times your shirt snags, and you stop to pull it free.

You tumble onto the deck into thick smoke. A British shell hits the deck and splinters into dozens of deadly fragments.

Men leap into the ocean. You're afraid to follow them into the thrashing waves without your life jacket. You look around desperately, wondering what to do.

• To look for a life raft, turn to page 143.

• To find a life jacket, turn to page 149.

You reach for a crutch and stand up. You hobble to the door of the sick bay. You are almost there when the ship lurches and tosses you onto the metal floor. Your head slams into a steel support.

When a medic rushes back to the sick bay for supplies, he finds your lifeless body curled against a metal locker. You won't be the only sailor to die on the *Bismarck* today.

THE END
To follow another path, turn to page 121.
To read the conclusion, turn to page 211.

The ship rocks back and forth. If you try to get up now, you're certain to fall. There's one explosion after another as the main guns blast the British ships. The British fire back. "The *Bismarck* is unsinkable," you tell yourself, but you're no longer sure you believe it. Smoke fills the sick bay. You try to sit up, but you're dizzy. You pull the blankets over your head to block the smoke.

In the engine room, Chief Engineer Walter Lehmann knows the ship can't be saved. He orders his men to sink the *Bismarck* by opening valves to let water into the hull. "It is better to sink our own ship than to let it fall into enemy hands." And so, amid a hail of British bombs and torpedoes, the mighty battleship slides into the ocean. You and hundreds of sailors die with her.

142

THE END

To follow another path, turn to page 121.
To read the conclusion, turn to page 211.

You turn to run, but the ship is tipping. The deck tilts under your feet and you slide toward the edge. You plunge feet-first into the icy water.

"Ahh!" you scream, struggling to catch your breath. Your legs and feet are numb with cold. As you thrash in the water, the British cruiser *Dorsetshire* steams toward you. British sailors lower ropes over the side. You begin pulling yourself up the rope, right into the hands of the British. They drag you over the railing, strip off your oil-soaked clothes, and wrap you in blankets.

You're surprised when they offer you hot tea and biscuits. These men are your enemies. Why are they being kind? Would you do the same for them?

Turn the page.

Most of the *Bismarck*'s crew were lost, but a few survivors were rescued by the Royal Navy's HMS *Dorsetshire*.

144

The *Dorsetshire* sails away with you aboard, leaving hundreds of German sailors in the water. A British sailor explains that German U-boats are nearby. You're relieved. Maybe the U-boats will save the others.

Eventually you are sent to a prisoner of war camp in Canada. When you return to Germany after the war, you take over your father's barbershop. You never return to the sea.

Years pass before you find Hans again. He'd been taken to a different camp. You are the lucky ones. Few of the *Bismarck*'s crew survived. You seldom talk about the war. There are too many sad memories.

145

THE END

To follow another path, turn to page 121.
To read the conclusion, turn to page 211.

Luck is with you. You shoot to the surface next to a life raft. A sailor helps you into the raft. You turn to look at the *Bismarck*. Flames dance along the deck. Some sailors jump into the sea. Others stand still, dazed and overwhelmed. The ship begins to tilt, and then the mighty *Bismarck* disappears into the sea. You can't believe it.

All day long your raft bobs on the waves. At 7:00 p.m. a German U-boat comes along. The sailors aboard pull you to safety. The sub searches for other survivors but finds none. You later learn that of the 2,206 men who sailed on the *Bismarck*, German ships rescued only five.

Every year on May 27, you salute the brave men who died on the *Bismarck*.

THE END
To follow another path, turn to page 121.
To read the conclusion, turn to page 211.

There's Hans! You both slide down the starboard hull to the keel and jump from there. "Swim!" he yells. "There's a British ship. They won't leave us here to drown."

That's when another sailor reaches out and grabs your life jacket. "Help me!" he says. "I can't swim!" He pulls you under.

"Let go!" you yell, but he holds even tighter. He thrashes around and pushes your head under the icy water. You struggle, but it's no use. You drown just a few yards from the British ship that rescues Hans.

147

THE END

To follow another path, turn to page 121.
To read the conclusion, turn to page 211.

It won't take long to go to the canteen for some hot food before you crawl into your bunk. "I'll bring you coffee too," you promise.

You're on your way to the canteen when a British plane flies over. Your mates begin firing their guns, but they aren't fast enough. The plane releases a torpedo. It slams into the hull right beside you. The blast throws you against a metal wall, snapping your neck. You become the first sailor to die on the battleship *Bismarck*. You won't be the last.

THE END

To follow another path, turn to page 121.
To read the conclusion, turn to page 211.

You run to get a life jacket. They're in a storage locker at the front of the ship. Devastation is everywhere. Fires burn along the length of the deck. The turrets are silent wrecks. But seeing the injured men is far worse. Some are missing legs or arms. Others hold their bleeding hands over gaping wounds.

A man reaches out for you. "Tell my girl I love her," he pleads just as a British shell slams into the deck. The blast knocks you down. A metal splinter pierces your neck. You die quickly with no time to think of the loved ones you're leaving behind.

149

THE END

To follow another path, turn to page 121.
To read the conclusion, turn to page 211.

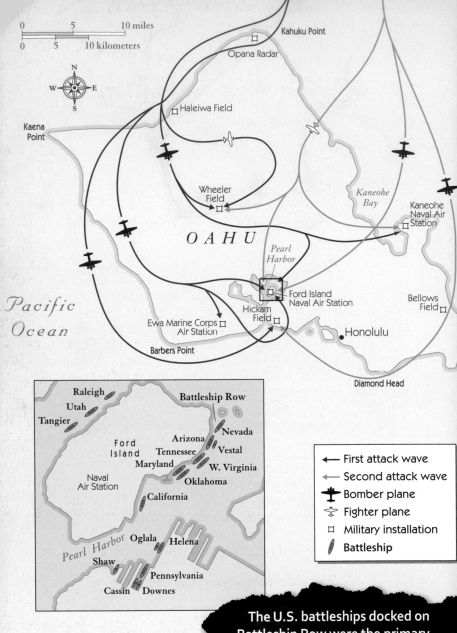

0 5 10 miles
0 5 10 kilometers

N
W E
S

Kahuku Point

Opana Radar

Haleiwa Field

Kaena
Point

Wheeler
Field

*Kaneohe
Bay*

Kaneohe
Naval Air
Station

O A H U

*Pearl
Harbor*

Ford Island
Naval Air Station

Bellows
Field

*Pacific
Ocean*

Ewa Marine Corps
Air Station

Hickam
Field

Honolulu

Barbers Point

Diamond Head

Raleigh
Utah
Tangier

Battleship Row

Nevada

*Ford
Island*

Arizona
Tennessee
Maryland

Vestal

W. Virginia

Naval
Air Station

Oklahoma

California

Pearl Harbor

Oglala

Helena

Shaw

Pennsylvania

Cassin Downes

← First attack wave
← Second attack wave
✈ Bomber plane
✈ Fighter plane
⬜ Military installation
⬭ Battleship

The U.S. battleships docked on
Battleship Row were the primary
targets of the Japanese raid.

CHAPTER 3

SURPRISE ATTACK

"I want to be a leatherneck," you tell your mother.

"A leatherneck?" she says, looking concerned.

"A United States Marine," you say proudly.

Before long it's time to leave for boot camp. It's tough saying good-bye. Mom cries and Dad hugs her. They both wave as you board the bus to San Diego, California.

Boot camp lasts seven weeks. You spend most of your time in close order drill. You learn to march, take and give orders, and handle a rifle. You also learn to set up camp and perform first aid. You receive special training in how to guard important people and places.

151

The drills are exhausting, the sergeant tough, and the beds uncomfortable. But by the end of boot camp you're ready to serve wherever and however you are needed.

In November 1941 you report to Pearl Harbor, Hawaii. It's the home base of the U.S. Navy's Pacific fleet. More than 90 ships are anchored there. Seven battleships line the southeast shore of Ford Island. "It's called Battleship Row," your buddy Jack says.

First in line is the *California.* Then several ships are moored side-by-side: *Maryland* with *Oklahoma,* and *Tennessee* with *West Virginia.* The *Arizona* is moored next to the repair ship *Vestal.* The *Nevada,* last in line, is all by herself. The eighth ship, the *Pennsylvania,* is in dry dock nearby for repairs.

You've always dreamed of serving on a battleship. You'll have the chance to sail the world. But if you work at the Marine base, you'll have the chance to explore Hawaii.

• To serve on a navy battleship, turn to page 154.

• To work at the Marine base, turn to page 158.

Eighty-seven Marines and nearly 1,500 sailors are assigned to the *Arizona*. You'll be guarding the brig, the gangplank, and other important areas of the ship. If there's a battle, you'll report to the superstructure deckhouse at the top of the ship. You'll man the 5-inch, 51-caliber guns that make up the secondary batteries.

For several weeks you practice battle drills at sea. On December 6 the *Arizona* returns to Pearl Harbor. On Sunday, December 7, you wake up early. As you're about to leave the breakfast table, the ship's siren for air defense sounds.

"We're being attacked!" a sailor yells.

You run to the port door in time to see a bomb strike a barge of some kind near the *Nevada*. Anti-aircraft guns fire back.

You climb the ladder on the starboard side of the ship near the tail. Your friend Harry follows. You scramble up another ladder to the second deck, past the Marines' compartment. One more ladder takes you above it and past one of the ship's casemates.

The casemate, an armored tower containing one of the ship's big guns, has a large window. It overlooks Ford Island and the battleship *Tennessee*. Harry stops to peer out. "Look!" he yells. "A Jap plane!"

You can see the Japanese flag on the underside of its wing. It drops something that looks oblong at first, and then becomes as round as a ball. It flashes into the sea about 100 yards from you. Whump! It's a bomb!

Turn the page.

Water splashes onto the deck. The ship lists 5 or 6 degrees toward the port side. You grab a railing to keep your balance. Did the bomb explode underwater? Did it damage the ship? You have no way to know. For the first time, the war feels real to you.

Ford Island had a navy yard for building and repairing ships, a naval air station, a hospital, and other facilities.

Another plane flies overhead. Boom! A torpedo strikes the ship. The *Arizona* rises out of the water. It then slams against the quay, the platform next to the ship for loading supplies. The impact sends men sprawling across the deck. The loudspeaker blares: "Japanese are attacking, all hands General Quarters." That means you have to get to your battle station in the main mast—now!

The *Arizona* has many decks and is as long as two football fields. But Harry stops at the bottom of the tripod mast leg because something is blocking his way. "It's Lieutenant Simonsen! He's been hit!" Harry kneels beside him.

157

• To help Harry with the lieutenant, turn to page 161.

• To report to your battle station, turn to page 163.

You're assigned to the Marine barracks at U.S. Navy headquarters. It's where the navy trains men for sea duty or to serve as guards at U.S. embassies around the world. You patrol the grounds, check identification papers, and do whatever it takes to keep order.

On December 6 you have liberty. You can do whatever you want. You decide to swim and surf at Waikiki Beach with your buddy Jack. It's great fun and an exciting change from life at home. Some sailors invite you to a luau. Beautiful girls dance the hula while musicians strum ukuleles. "This is the life," you say. "I could stay here forever."

"Too bad we have to be back on base by 11 o'clock," Jack says.

The next morning, December 7, you wake up at 7:00. "Why so early?" Jack asks, yawning.

"I promised my mother I'd go to church. So did you." You shower and shave. "Let's go. We'll get coffee and a doughnut on the way."

But you never make it off the base. A few minutes before 8:00, you hear an explosion. Bullets punch holes in the barracks roof. "We're under attack!" Sergeant Wilson yells, but you barely hear him over the drumming of the bullets and the panic of your mates.

"Attack? But the United States isn't at war!"

Several bombers fly overhead. The red circles under the wings represent the Japanese flag. You call them meatballs.

159

Turn the page.

"It's the Japanese," Sarge says. "And they're headed for Battleship Row." That's where the navy's big battleships dock. You run down the hallway and grab a rifle from the gun rack. So does Jack.

Sarge leads you to a retaining wall that provides some cover. "When I give the command, fire!" What good is a rifle against a bomber? But before you can shoot, Sarge yells, "Hold your fire!"

A lone sailor is trying to set up a machine gun about 100 feet away. "That man needs help," Sarge yells. You'll have to cross an open patch of ground to reach him.

• To volunteer to help the sailor, turn to page 169.

• To stay with Sarge, turn to page 173.

You stop to help the lieutenant, but it's too late. He's dying. He motions for you to continue up the ladder.

You climb the ladders on the tripod mast to your battle station. Japanese machine gunners fire down on you. Bullets ping off the ship's metal armor and chip the paint around you.

A bomb hits the quarterdeck, creating a large hole. You reach your battle station, but there's not much you can do. Your guns are no use against the Japanese bombers.

161

Turn the page.

You look out over Ford Field, where navy planes smoke and burn. The sky is filled with Japanese planes bombing other battleships along Battleship Row. The shock of the attack silences the men around you.

Then a Japanese bomb crashes into the bow of the ship. It explodes in the powder magazine, setting off the ammunition stored there. The ship shakes, lurches, and rises out of the water before it explodes.

You're tossed onto the deck. The smell of burning oil wraps itself around you like a heavy blanket. You're tempted to take cover behind one of the ship's steel supports. But if you can get below, maybe you can reach the gangplank and escape.

• To go below, turn to page 165.

• To take cover, turn to page 166.

It's your job to get to your battle station. You are climbing toward it when you hear a loud whooshing sound. That sound is followed by a series of explosions. Torpedoes have hit the ship below water level.

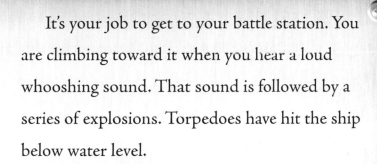

All eight U.S. battleships at Pearl Harbor were either sunk or badly damaged.

Turn the page.

A bomb goes directly down one of the gun turrets. The powder magazine, where ammunition is stored, explodes. The *Arizona* shakes. Men tumble onto the deck. Smoke swirls around you. The ship—what's left of it—is on fire! The battle is less than 20 minutes old.

You begin climbing down the ladder toward the gangplank. You have to get off the ship! You're nearly there when a torpedo explodes on the battleship *Nevada*. The explosion makes the *Arizona* bounce around like a toy boat. An officer orders, "Abandon ship!"

But where's Harry? You need to get off the ship, but you can't leave your friend behind.

• To abandon ship, turn to page 167.

• To look for Harry, turn to page 181.

You go below. By the time you reach the quarterdeck, the heat is intense. Badly burned sailors move past you like zombies. Most are beyond help.

The ship's mooring lines pull tight against the weight of the sinking ship. In a few more minutes they'll break. The ship will go down. The gangplank has flipped sideways. To cross, you'll have to walk along a 2-inch-wide strip of plank to the quay, the platform used to load and unload supplies.

If you can get across, you'll be safe—at least for a while. You're about to step onto the plank when someone calls your name. Is it Harry?

• To turn around, turn to page 168.

• To keep going, turn to page 175.

You run along the deck. There's the gangplank! You're almost to safety. But the deck is slick with the blood of wounded men. As you race forward, you fall and slide toward the railing. You try to grab something—anything—but you keep sliding. Another bomb hits the ship. The next thing you know, you're in the water.

Navy sailors were able to rescue a few men from the water during the attacks.

Turn to page 171.

You make a dash for the steps leading belowdecks. You stumble down them and head for the gangplank. "Hurry!" a sailor says. "This gangplank is about to give way." It sways wildly as you cross to the quay.

The only way to shore from the quay is to swim. You dive into the chilly water and swim past globs of oil, pieces of metal and wood, and even dead bodies. Finally you climb ashore and collapse. Some men are crying. Others, like you, feel stunned and dazed as they watch the mighty battleships burn.

Turn to page 177.

"Harry?" you call, but you can't see him. Meanwhile, another Marine moves ahead of you. He's halfway across when a cable near the gangplank snaps. The jolt knocks the sailor into the water below.

"Let's go!" someone behind you yells. You hold your breath and force yourself across the gangplank to the quay.

Several small boats are moored there. Joe, one of the ship's carpenters, is trying to start a boat. But he seems confused. You don't know how to handle the boat either.

"Get in," he says. But it might be safer to swim.

• To swim ashore, turn to page 171.

• To get into the boat, turn to page 174.

"I'll go!" you shout. Jack goes too. Planes fly overhead, and bullets spray the dirt around you. You've never run so fast in your life. The machine gun sits next to an ammo shed. It offers little protection against the raining bullets. You and Jack help the sailor set up and load the gun.

"Hold it steady!" You aim the gun toward a bomber. Jack gives the command. "Ready, aim, fire!"

The Japanese bomber explodes. "That's one less meatball!" Jack yells.

169

Turn the page.

You fire until you're out of ammunition. That's when fear takes over. Your country may not be officially at war, but you're in the middle of a major battle. Your hands shake. You're excited and scared at the same time. Reading about war in the newspaper is different from living it.

The attack stops suddenly. Sergeant Wilson says, "Form two groups. One group will stay here and man the guns. The other will go to the dock to help the wounded."

• To help the wounded, turn to page 178.

• To man the guns, turn to page 180.

Waves slap you in the face, choking you. Bits of steel and pieces of wood slosh past you in the choppy water. You see a buoy and grab onto it. Wave after wave of Japanese planes passes overhead, dropping bombs and spraying bullets. The sky lights up like a fireworks display. But it's not fireworks—it's the *Arizona*.

All the ammunition, guns, and shells are exploding in a series of roars, pops, and booms. Oil and bits of twisted metal from the damaged ships float past.

For a while, the attack stops. You begin the mile-long swim to shore. By the time you get there, you're exhausted and covered with oil and sludge. Your uniform has turned black. So have your skin and hair. But you're safe. You survived.

171

Turn the page.

Every year on December 7 you remember the 2,403 sailors and civilians who weren't as lucky. You'll never forget the sacrifice they made.

THE END
To follow another path, turn to page 121.
To read the conciusion, turn to page 211.

You hate to admit it, but you're scared. Even Sarge looks worried. Another man volunteers to help with the machine gun. You feel safer behind the retaining wall. When the next plane passes over, you aim for the red circle on the wing.

"Ready, aim, fire!" Sarge yells. You fire a rifle. Others shoot pistols as the machine gun rattles out bullets. The plane explodes. "Hurray! We got one!"

The bombing stops as quickly as it began. An officer sends you to guard the main gate at Marine headquarters. You hear explosions in the distance and sirens whining, but the worst seems to be over.

173

Turn to page 177.

The water is full of oil, sludge, and dead bodies. You can't imagine trying to swim through it, so you take a chance on the boat. But Joe is struggling to control the boat.

"Give me the wheel!" another man yells. A fight breaks out. When you stand up to stop the fight, you're knocked overboard. Your head smashes into a steel beam. You sink below the churning water, a victim of the surprise Japanese attack on Pearl Harbor.

THE END

To follow another path, turn to page 121.
To read the conclusion, turn to page 211.

You don't stop. You have to escape the burning ship. You're halfway across the gangplank when one of the heavy cables between the ship and the quay snaps. The jolt knocks you off the plank. You hit the side of the sinking ship with a thud. You slip beneath the surface of the water, unconscious. You'll be counted among the 2,403 who died in the attack on Pearl Harbor.

THE END

To follow another path, turn to page 121.
To read the conclusion, turn to page 211.

176

Air Force planes and hangars at nearby Hickam Field were also targeted by Japanese bombers.

You're shaken, but alive. You're assigned to the *Maryland* as a security officer. She was luckier than most of the ships on Battleship Row. Only two bombs hit the *Maryland*, causing light damage.

By February 1942 the ship returns to active service with you on board. You return home when the war ends in 1945, but you never forget what happened at Pearl Harbor on December 7, 1941.

177

THE END

To follow another path, turn to page 121.
To read the conclusion, turn to page 211.

You run to the water's edge. The men who jumped from the battleships are coated with oil and slime. Some are badly injured, burned, or missing limbs. You feel sick. You force down your fear and help them out of the water.

You pull several men to shore. An ambulance roars up. Medics whisk the men away. Many will not survive their injuries. More bodies float in the water. Pulling them out is the saddest thing you've ever done.

A second attack begins. Planes drop bombs and spray the ground with bullets. You look toward the battleships and see the great *Oklahoma* flop onto its side. The *Arizona* explodes.

The next three days pass in a blur. There's no time to do anything but follow orders. Finally you steal a minute to send a message home. Your telegram is just two words: "Am Safe." It's the best news your mother has ever received. She treasures it as long as she lives.

THE END

To follow another path, turn to page 121.
To read the conclusion, turn to page 211.

You and Jack man the machine gun. "Another attack may come at any moment," the sergeant says.

"We need more ammo," you say. You offer to dash across the open area to the shed where the ammunition is stored. As you run to the shed, another bomber flies over. This time you're the target. A bullet strikes you in the leg. You stumble and fall but are able to crawl to safety.

You're treated on the hospital ship *Solace* and then transferred to a military hospital on the mainland. For the rest of your life, you walk with a limp. But you consider yourself lucky. You made it home safely—unlike thousands of others who died in the attack on Pearl Harbor.

180

THE END

To follow another path, turn to page 121.
To read the conclusion, turn to page 211.

"Harry!" you call, but it's impossible to hear anything over the explosions. You zigzag past fires, debris, and injured men to the place where you last saw Harry. He's resting against a metal support. "Over here, pal," he calls. He's gripping his stomach, trying to stop the flow of blood.

"I took a hit," he says. "Will you write my mom? Tell her I love her."

You grab Harry under his arms. "I'll get you out of here."

But it's too late. Harry dies in your arms. Moments later a Japanese plane buzzes overhead, raining bullets onto the burning deck. One of them hits you. You collapse and die on the deck of the burning *Arizona* next to your pal Harry.

THE END
To follow another path, turn to page 121.
To read the conclusion, turn to page 211.

181

Navy sailors were briefed before beginning the D-Day invasion.

CHAPTER 4

INVASION

Mother's voice is shaking as she reads the headline out loud: "U.S. Declares War; Military Casualties Total Almost 2,500." She puts down the newspaper and shakes her head.

"I'm joining the navy," you say.

"Not until you graduate from high school," Mother insists.

For the next two years you read about the war, put battle maps on your bedroom wall, and talk to anyone who has ever served as a sailor. The day after high school graduation, you enlist in the navy.

183

Turn the page.

The navy barber shaves your head. It's called a buzz cut. You are issued a uniform, a hammock with a mattress and two blankets, and a seabag to carry it all.

They call you a "boot" and give you *The Bluejackets' Manual*. "Study it!" Chief Petty Officer Rogers says. But after a day of doing sit-ups, marching, and rifle training, you're too tired to do much reading.

One day Chief Rogers says, "We need men to serve in the amphibious force. You'll learn to handle an LCM, which is a landing craft, mechanized. It takes men and equipment from ship to shore." You like the sound of that, so you volunteer.

At the training center in Little Creek, Virginia, you're assigned to an LCM 6, a 56-foot steel boat. It takes four men to handle the LCM. The coxswain controls the boat and the motor mac repairs the engine. You and another bowman, Tom, stand watch to make sure the LCM doesn't hit any obstacles. There's no armor on the open deck to protect you from enemy bullets.

When your training is finished, you go to England to prepare for a secret landing in Europe. Everyone is excited. This is the big invasion you've been waiting for. If the landing goes well, the Allies can begin marching across Europe.

Turn the page.

On June 5, 1944, you receive orders to cross the English Channel to France. "In another 12 hours we'll send the troop carriers across," Captain Orr, one of the commanding officers, says. "We want the landing craft ready to take soldiers from ships to shore."

The sea is choppy. Waves 10 to 12 feet high rock the LCM. It's 5:30 a.m. when you reach the area 11 miles offshore where U.S. troop carriers are anchored. A boat officer directs you to pull alongside one of the carriers.

Eighty navy bomb experts board the LCM. The men fill every bit of space in the LCM. "It's like being packed in an open tin can," Tom says. Each man carries two packs of explosives. On shore they'll blow up the bridges and roads. That should stop the German Army!

Army troops crowded onto a landing craft headed to Normandy.

187

Turn the page.

You head for Omaha Beach. The beach is crowded with crafts trying to land. But you manage to drop off the troops and go back for a second load.

During the second trip, you are carrying a group of army infantrymen to shore. German snipers begin firing down at you from machine gun nests on the cliffs above! You have no weapons or protection in the open boat. Bullets pelt the deck. Your instincts tell you to cower and protect yourself, but that won't help.

188

You ignore the danger and do what you've been trained to do—get the troops to shore. But you think you see something just under the water ahead. You're the bowman. It's up to you to tell the coxswain to back off or push forward.

- *To back off, go to page 189.*
- *To push forward, turn to page 190.*

You give the "back off" signal to the coxswain. The Germans have rigged mines offshore to protect this 6-mile stretch of Omaha Beach from invasion. You recall the officer's warning: "Be alert. If you hit a mine, it will destroy the LCM and everyone on it."

Luckily this obstacle isn't a mine. It's an overturned tank that fell off a landing craft. The coxswain swerves to the right, and the LCM moves forward. But the conditions are getting worse. Fog and smoke from gunfire block your view. Waves rock the boat. The bullets keep coming. "We need to get these men ashore!" Lieutenant Johnson yells. "Lower the ramp!"

"But, sir, the water's too rough and deep," you reply.

• To lower the ramp, turn to page 191.

• To wait, turn to page 193.

189

The lieutenant in charge orders you forward. His men want to get to shore. But do they know that the Germans have planted explosives in the water? If you hit a mine, the LCM will be blown to bits.

You hold your breath as you continue forward. Then you sigh in relief. It's not a mine—just a tank that fell off a larger landing craft. You're safe, this time.

The troops plunge into the icy water and wade ashore. You're about to return to the ship for more troops when another landing craft loses control in the waves. It tips over. Men struggle in the deep water, weighed down by their gear. If you rescue them, you'll be a target for the German gunners firing from the bluff above.

• To rescue the men in the water, turn to page 195.

• To return to the ship, turn to page 196.

Lieutenant Johnson insists. You and Tom lower the ramp. Rough water forces the ramp to buck up and slam back down. The first man off can't get out of the way in time. The ramp smacks him in the head. "Ow!" he yells. "That could have killed me."

"Jump off the sides!" Johnson orders, leading the way. The men follow and begin wading through water reaching their armpits. One soldier is seasick. He throws up and drops his helmet.

"You can't go ashore without a helmet," you say, giving him yours. He salutes you as he jumps off the LCM. He may be an army man, but he's wearing a navy helmet when he storms Omaha Beach.

191

Turn the page.

Several men make it safely to shore. Others struggle against the waves. As you're backing up, you see a soldier who's having trouble staying afloat in the water. He's several feet below you. Reaching out to him will put you in danger, especially since you gave your helmet away.

Army troops waded to Omaha Beach from a landing craft.

• To help the man, turn to page 194.

• To keep going, turn to page 202.

"Give us a minute," you say. "If we can get in closer, you'll be safer." Lieutenant Johnson agrees. You lower the ramp a few feet closer to shore. The troops all make it off the LCM, but they have to duck German bullets on their way to shore. The water is full of wounded men. You rescue those within easy reach and take them back to the ships. The medics will help them.

When you return from your sixth run, Captain Orr directs you to a Liberty ship. Liberty ships carry supplies. They hold more than 9,000 tons of cargo. That equals 2,840 jeeps, 440 tanks, or 230 million rounds of rifle ammunition. Captain Bunker, the Liberty ship captain, greets you and invites you on board for a hot meal. But you have work to do.

- *To accept a meal, turn to page 199.*
- *To return to duty, turn to page 204.*

193

You reach out to the soldier with a pole. He grabs it and pulls so hard that you lose your balance and fall overboard. The water is littered with packs, guns, and clothing. Worst of all are the bodies of soldiers killed as they tried to make it to shore.

You can't find the soldier you were trying to help. You reach the shore and take cover behind an overturned tank. German bullets ping off of it.

A soldier a few feet from you is hit and tumbles backward. His rifle falls nearby. You can't help him, but you may be able to reach his gun. You glance out at the sea. Is that your LCM still in the landing zone?

194

• To run for the LCM, turn to page 197.

• To reach for the rifle, turn to page 201.

The overturned LCM is close to yours, so you call to the men. "Over here! We can help!" Several are able to swim within reach. You pull one soldier out of the water. Several of his buddies follow. Many are injured. The German guns are still firing. Without any weapons, you feel as if a big target is painted on the LCM's deck. You've stayed too long. Luckily most of the men have clambered aboard.

"Let's go!" you shout. You look over the side and see a dark shape beneath the water. It could be the LCM's shadow. Or it could be a German mine.

195

• To ignore the shadow, turn to page 205.

• To check for mines, turn to page 206.

Leaving those men in the water is one of the toughest things you've ever done. Tom senses your concern. "Some of them will make it on their own," he says. "And the more troops we transport, the better our chance of victory."

You carry troops and equipment ashore for two days. The battle has moved inland and the beach is secured. As you make a final landing, the LCM scrapes against an overturned tank and is damaged. The coxswain beaches the LCM. "This will take a while," the motor mac says. "You boys may as well have a look around."

You and Tom climb one of the cliffs. At the top you find a German "pillbox." It's a concrete shelter designed to hold a machine gun and several soldiers. There's a small steel door.

• To open the door, turn to page 208.

• To leave it alone, turn to page 209.

It is your LCM! You dodge bullets as you zigzag across the sand and swim toward it. The tide is coming in. The water pushes against you as you swim. You reach the LCM and climb on just before Tom closes the ramp.

"Thought we lost you," Tom says.

You take healthy soldiers to shore and wounded soldiers back to the ship all day long. You lose track of how many trips you've made before darkness makes it impossible to continue. By that time, you're exhausted.

The coxswain drops anchor far from the beach. You eat K rations and set up your cot on the deck of the LCM. You try to block the horrible images of the dead and wounded from your mind.

Turn the page.

An amphibious vehicle called an LST (landing ship, tank) unloaded British tanks and trucks for the attack.

You transport soldiers to the beach for two more days. When the troops move inland, your work eases up.

Turn to page 207.

A hot meal sounds great. The steaming plate of steak and eggs is the best food you've had in weeks. What's the catch?

You learn soon enough. The Liberty ship is loaded with ammunition. "We're setting up an ammo dump on the beach," Captain Bunker says. "Now that we've taken the beach, the army will begin the long march across France to Germany. They'll need plenty of ammo to fight the Germans." They begin loading up your LCM.

After the short trip to shore carrying the ammo, army troops unload the LCM. While they're working, you and your mates wander onto the bluffs. This is where German machine gunners fired down on you during the invasion. The machine gun nests are burned out, the guns silenced, and their operators killed in action.

Turn the page.

The beach is an Allied military post now. Jeeps, trucks, and tanks lumber along the sand. They'll carry supplies to the Allied armies. Your job here is done. Soon you'll be sent for more training. Then you'll head to the Pacific to assist with the invasion of Japanese-held islands.

There will be more battles, but it is this battle that you'll remember most clearly. You'll never forget the brave soldiers who stormed the beaches of Normandy on D-Day.

THE END
To follow another path, turn to page 121.
To read the conclusion, turn to page 211.

The rifle is so close. But you have to leave the safety of the overturned tank to grab it. You're only exposed to gunfire for a few seconds, but that's all it takes for a German bullet to strike your leg. You crawl back to the tank. You stay hidden for hours, clenching your teeth against the pain until a medic rescues you.

You spend the next few months in a navy hospital in Virginia. You follow the progress of the war, knowing that you helped the Allies to victory. You only wish you could have done more.

201

THE END

To follow another path, turn to page 121.
To read the conclusion, turn to page 211.

Lots of men are struggling. You'd like to help them all, but your job is to get more troops to shore. You speed back to the troop carrier. On your third trip to the beach, waves are so high that you can't get close enough to release the ramp. Finally an officer jumps over the side. "Let's go!" he orders. The men hold their guns over their heads and wade to shore. German bullets batter the LCM and strike men in the water. Two soldiers are hit as they jump off the LCM. You reach out and pull them back on board.

At the same moment, a bullet hits Tom. "Tom!" You rush forward, but Tom pushes you away. "I'm OK," he says. "The bullet only grazed me. I'm fine."

You turn to signal the coxswain, and that's when a bullet strikes you. But it doesn't just graze you—it pierces your chest and kills you instantly.

The LCM carries your body back to the troop carrier with the other dead and wounded. For you, the war is over.

LCMs carried dead and injured troops from the beaches back to the ships.

THE END

To follow another path, turn to page 121.
To read the conclusion, turn to page 211.

"Maybe later," you say. "We have to report to the boat director first." You make many trips carrying men and supplies. As night falls, you drop anchor and eat your K rations. You and your crew sleep on cots on the open deck of the LCM. At least you're safe—far from shore and near the transport carrier.

After six days at Normandy, you load the LCM onto a transport ship. You're headed back to the United States. Your commander has ordered you to Florida for advanced training on amphibious landing crafts. The war is still raging in the Pacific. You'll probably go there next.

By the end of 1944, France is free of German control. You helped make that happen.

THE END
To follow another path, turn to page 121.
To read the conclusion, turn to page 211.

You signal the coxswain, "Go!" The water is full of clothing, lost weapons, bodies, and even an overturned tank. The dark shadow you're seeing is probably just debris from earlier landings. After all, navy minesweepers cleared the area earlier.

But morning came before the minesweepers finished the job. When your LCM moves forward, it sets off a German mine that the minesweepers missed. It explodes. Steel balls and metal fragments spray the area. One hits you. You don't even have time to realize your mistake.

205

THE END

To follow another path, turn to page 121.
To read the conclusion, turn to page 211.

"I'll check it out," you say. You dive off the end of the ramp and search beneath the LCM until you find the obstacle. "It's a mine!" you yell as Tom helps you on board. The coxswain steers away, and the LCM safely delivers the wounded men to a troop carrier.

For the next few days, you carry supplies to shore. The army has moved on, and the beach is secure. The Germans are on the run.

German sailors planted mines that lay just below the water's surface, ready to detonate.

"You did well, men," Captain Orr says. "You played an important role in our victory."

Years later you tell your grandchildren about your experience in World War II. You tell them about the brave men who gave their lives on that faraway beach so that others could live in freedom.

THE END
To follow another path, turn to page 121.
To read the conclusion, turn to page 211.

You open the door. A German soldier peers back at you! You jump backward, and the German slams the door shut. You run to find an officer.

"There are no Germans left here," Lieutenant Blake scoffs.

"I'll bet you $5 there are," you say.

"You're on!" Lieutenant Blake bangs on the door. No answer. He fires a shot down a ventilation hole. Still no response. Finally he sends the soldiers for explosives and blows the door open. Fifteen German soldiers walk out. They're stunned by the blast but not hurt. Blake's men take the Germans prisoner.

Lieutenant Blake hands you a $5 bill. But the real prize comes later. You receive the Bronze Star for capturing 15 German prisoners of war.

THE END

To follow another path, turn to page 121.
To read the conclusion, turn to page 211.

208

The Germans are gone. There's no point in opening the door. Besides, it's time to return to the beach. When you get back, the LCM is repaired and ready to go. The next day you take more equipment to shore.

One day as you are loading a large gun onto the LCM, a cable breaks. It throws you into the ocean. Tom pulls you out of the water, but your leg is badly damaged. By the time you recover, the war has ended. You return home from the naval hospital full of stories of D-Day and your role in the amphibious navy.

209

THE END

To follow another path, turn to page 121.
To read the conclusion, turn to page 211.

The crewmen of the USS *Ward* showed off their scorecard of successful battles.

CHAPTER 5

A RECORD-BREAKING WAR

Navies played a major role in World War II. Sailors and Marines served on battleships, in submarines, and on the landing crafts that carried soldiers from ship to shore. Battles took place in the Atlantic and Pacific oceans, the Mediterranean Sea, and many smaller waterways.

One of the first major naval battles occurred in May 1941 when the German battleship *Bismarck* sank Great Britain's HMS *Hood*. The battle between the two giant ships lasted only 8 minutes before the *Hood* burned and sank.

The British fleet rushed to the scene. On the morning of May 27, British ships fired 2,800 shells at the *Bismarck*. Four hundred shells hit the target and destroyed the mighty ship. Only 116 of the 2,206 German sailors survived. British ships rescued 111. Those men became prisoners of war. German boats found five more survivors.

A few months later, on Sunday, December 7, 1941, the Japanese launched an attack on the U.S. Navy fleet at Pearl Harbor. Nearly 200 Japanese torpedo planes, bombers, and fighters fired on the U.S. battleships on Battleship Row. The attack surprised everyone.

The battleship *Arizona* was destroyed. The *Oklahoma* capsized. The *California, Nevada,* and *West Virginia* sank in shallow water. On the *Arizona*, 1,177 crewmen lost their lives. There were 2,403 Americans killed in the Pearl Harbor attack. Another 1,100 were injured. The next day the U.S. Congress declared war on Japan. The United States began fighting the Axis powers.

Meanwhile the Germans were gaining territory in Europe. France had fallen to the Germans. So had Norway, the Netherlands, and many other countries. The Allies wanted to land troops on the coast of Western Europe. British, Canadian, and American military leaders spent two years planning the invasion, called Operation Overlord. People would come to know it as D-Day.

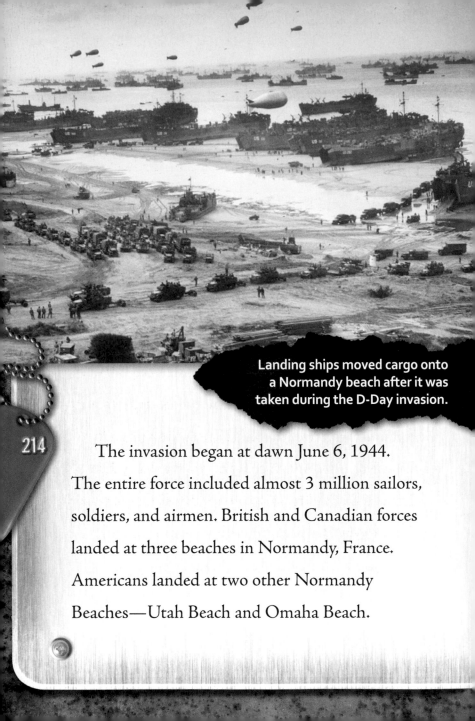

Landing ships moved cargo onto a Normandy beach after it was taken during the D-Day invasion.

The invasion began at dawn June 6, 1944. The entire force included almost 3 million sailors, soldiers, and airmen. British and Canadian forces landed at three beaches in Normandy, France. Americans landed at two other Normandy Beaches—Utah Beach and Omaha Beach.

More than 6,400 ships and landing craft brought 156,000 soldiers to the area. The sailors who operated the landing craft were key to the operation's success. The D-Day landing helped the Allies to victory. Germany surrendered on May 8, 1945.

The war in the Pacific continued for several more months. Many men who had served at Pearl Harbor or Normandy also served in the Pacific. World War II finally ended September 2, 1945, when Japan surrendered. Between 40 million and 50 million people were killed as a direct result of the conflict. No other war in world history has claimed more lives or spanned more territory than World War II.

TIMELINE

1939—Germany invades Poland September 1.

On **September 3** Great Britain, France, Australia, and New Zealand declare war on Germany.

President Franklin D. Roosevelt declares the United States neutral **September 5**.

1940—Germany invades Norway and Denmark **April 9**.

On **May 10** Germany invades France, the Netherlands, Belgium, and Luxembourg.

The Battle of Britain begins in **July**.

Roosevelt establishes a required draft in the United States **September 16**.

On **September 27** Germany, Italy, and Japan unite as the Axis powers.

1941—German battleship *Bismarck* sinks the British battleship *Hood* **May 24**.

On **May 27** British ships destroy the *Bismarck*.

Japan bombs Pearl Harbor, Hawaii, **December 7**.

On **December 8** the United States declares war on Japan.

1942—In spring the mass murder of Jews begins at Auschwitz concentration camp in Poland.

U.S. forces land on Guadalcanal in the Pacific **August 7**.

1943—Allies land in Sicily **July 9–10**.

Italy surrenders to the Allies **September 3**.

1944 On **June 6** D-Day invasion begins at Normandy, France.

The Battle of the Bulge begins in France **December 16**.

1945—On **February 19** U.S. forces land on Iwo Jima, off the coast of Japan.

The Allies reach Germany **March 7**.

On **April 1** U.S. forces invade the Japanese island of Okinawa.

Germany surrenders to the Allies **May 8**.

The United States drops an atomic bomb on Hiroshima, Japan, **August 6**.

On **August 9** the United States drops a second atomic bomb—this time on Nagasaki, Japan.

On **September 2** Japan surrenders. World War II ends.

OTHER PATHS TO EXPLORE

In this book you've seen how the events of the past look different from three points of view. Perspectives on history are as varied as the people who lived it. Seeing history from many points of view is an important part of understanding it.

Here are some ideas for other World War II points of view to explore:

+ Navy nurses served on the hospital ships *Solace* and *Relief* to provide medical help to wounded sailors. What would it have been like to work in one of the floating hospitals?

+ During World War II the sailors of the U.S. Coast Guard not only guarded the U.S. coasts, but also went to war against German submarines. The U.S. Navy credited the Coast Guard with sinking or helping to sink 13 German submarines, called U-boats. What would it have been like to battle a German U-boat?

+ Serving on a submarine required special training and the ability to live in tight quarters beneath the sea. What would it have been like to spend weeks at a time underwater?

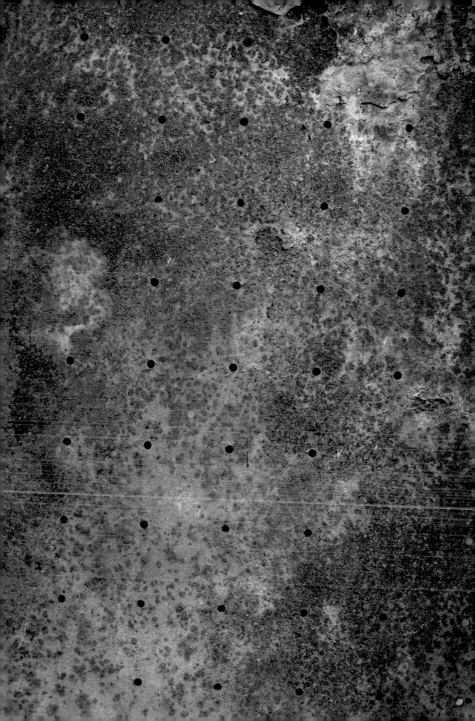

WORLD WAR II PILOTS:

AN INTERACTIVE HISTORY ADVENTURE

BY MICHAEL BURGAN

CONSULTANT:
DENNIS SHOWALTER, PHD
PROFESSOR OF HISTORY
COLORADO COLLEGE

TABLE OF CONTENTS

ABOUT YOUR ADVENTURE

YOU are living through World War II. It's the early 1940s, and airplanes, including bombers and fighters, are playing a major role in battle. You want to join the fight.

In this book you'll explore how the choices people made meant the difference between life and death. The events you'll experience happened to real people.

Chapter One sets the scene. Then you choose which path to read. Follow the directions at the bottom of each page. The choices you make will change your outcome. After you finish your path, go back and read the others for new perspectives and more adventures.

YOU CHOOSE the path
you take through history.

WARFARE IN THE SKIES

World War II started in 1939 and involves dozens of countries. The war's roots are deep, going back to the end of World War I in 1918.

In World War I the winning countries called themselves the Allies. They blamed Germany for starting the war and wanted to punish it afterward. Germany had to give up some of its land and its military. The Allies, particularly France and Great Britain, also demanded that Germany pay for the damage it caused during the war.

225

Turn the page.

Through the 1920s Germany became angry over this treatment. In 1933 a new leader came to power in Germany—Adolf Hitler. He promised to make Germany a strong, powerful nation again. He also wanted to punish people he thought had weakened Germany. This included the country's Jewish citizens. He and his Nazi Party took away Jews' legal rights and sent them to prison camps.

Through the 1930s Germany secretly strengthened its military—including building a huge new air force. Then, starting in 1936, Hitler sent troops into parts of Europe where Germans lived, claiming the land for his country. Germany's invasion of Poland in September 1939 marked the beginning of World War II.

German soldiers marched in a victory parade after the invasion of Poland.

Italy, which became a partner of Germany, also wanted to spread its control. Italian leader Benito Mussolini sent troops into part of North Africa. In Asia, Japan was making a similar grab for new land. The Japanese, like the Germans and Italians, thought they had the right to rule other countries.

Turn the page.

By 1939 military planners around the world saw airplanes as a key weapon. Planes were used to bring troops into battle as well as attack enemy forces. And the development of aircraft carriers—ships that carry aircraft—meant planes could carry out attacks far in the ocean.

On December 7, 1941, Japanese warplanes bombed the U.S. naval base at Pearl Harbor, Hawaii. The planes killed more than 2,000 Americans. The United States quickly declared war on Japan. Japan's partners, Italy and Germany, then declared war on the United States.

The countries of Germany, Italy, and Japan are known as the Axis powers. The Allies in this war are countries that oppose the Axis, including the United States, France, Poland, Great Britain, and many others as the war progresses.

As the war builds, you feel called to duty. You want to help defend your country—and you want to do it in the skies. You decide to become a pilot.

• *To be a British pilot in the Royal Air Force, turn to page 231.*

• *To be an American pilot fighting in the Pacific Ocean, turn to page 259.*

• *To be a member of the Tuskegee Airmen, turn to page 291.*

229

Firefighters put out flames from German bombs during the Battle of Britain.

CHAPTER 2

THE BATTLE OF BRITAIN

It's September 1939 and your town in Great Britain is in an uproar. German troops invaded Poland, and British leaders have promised to help the Poles. Your country declares war on Germany.

Your parents have heard the news about the war. Your father tells you, "With the war coming, you have to sign up for National Service. That means you could be called up for the military."

"I know," you say. "But I don't want to wait. I want to volunteer for the Royal Air Force."

"A pilot!" your mother wails. "Why do you want to risk your life in the RAF?"

"You know I've always wanted to fly," you reply.

231

Turn the page.

Your mother fights back tears and looks at your father. "He could ask for a deferment, since we need him here on the farm," your father says. Your mother nods and looks at you.

You know your parents count on you. But so does your country. Germany might even invade Britain some day, just like it did Poland. You want to defend your homeland.

• *To seek a deferment, go to page 233.*

• *To volunteer for the RAF, turn to page 238.*

Your deferment is approved, but you still often think about flying. Not much fighting takes place in Europe for the rest of the year. Then in the spring of 1940, Hitler's armies begin to move again. On the radio you hear about the invasion of Norway and Denmark. Next, Belgium and the Netherlands are captured. And by June the Germans have taken France as well. You wonder if Britain will be next.

An attack finally comes in August. German planes attack the RAF aerodrome at Manston Air Base. Germany's continued air assault is soon known as the Battle of Britain. Soon the Germans have changed their targets. Instead of bombing military bases like Manston, they've switched to Britain's largest cities, including London.

Turn the page.

You decide you have to act. You volunteer for the RAF and begin training. Just as you had hoped, you're learning to fly a fighter plane. And what a plane it is—the Spitfire, the newest and fastest British fighter. In it, you can soar at more than 350 miles per hour. You pass all your tests, are assigned to your squadron, and begin flying in missions.

The Spitfire's great speed allowed it to fly deep into enemy territory and escape quickly.

After a recent mission, you told the mechanic, Burt, that your engine wasn't working right. You've got another mission today, but Burt hasn't had time to fix it yet. You probably shouldn't fly it. "Maybe you can take Henderson's plane," Burt says. "He's too sick to fly."

You know exactly how your plane flies. You'll feel more comfortable in it. But it could be dangerous to fly before it is repaired.

235

• To take Henderson's plane, turn to page 236.

• To fly your own plane, turn to page 244.

You climb into Henderson's plane, take off down the runway, and head for the German planes approaching the coast. A voice comes in over your radio. "Bandits at 5,000 feet," the controller says, referring to enemy planes. "Looks like Me 109s."

"I see them," you say. You line up the closest Messerschmitt 109 in your gun sight and press the gun button. Nothing happens! You press again and again, but still no bullets. In the confusion of switching to Henderson's plane, the armorer forgot to load the machine guns!

You turn again as the Me 109 shoots at you. Some of the bullets rip into your plane. They don't cause serious damage, though, and you fly on. But you can't do much to stop the Me 109s if you don't have any bullets.

You're just about to head back to base when you see one of the enemy planes closing in on another Spitfire. You know the pilot—Archie Nelson. You want to help him, but you're not sure what you can do without bullets.

237

• To try to help Archie, turn to page 247.

• To go back to base, turn to page 250.

You look at your parents. "I'm sorry, Mum, Dad," you say. "I'm going to join the RAF."

You start weeks of training in the classroom. Each day starts before 6 a.m. You study math and learn how to navigate. Outside, you do fast marches across the camp or go on long runs. You face extra drills outside if you disobey any rules.

Through all this early training, you don't even get inside a plane. And you still have more weeks ahead in the classroom. You begin to wonder if you've made the right decision. Maybe you should have asked for that deferment.

238

• To stay in the RAF, go to page 239.

• To leave the RAF, turn to page 252.

You decide to work harder. After classroom training, you go to a new base where you finally start to fly. You climb into a Tiger Moth, a biplane designed to teach new pilots. An instructor flies with you in a second cockpit. After just 15 flight hours with him, he lets you fly solo.

After several months more training, you earn your wings—you're an RAF pilot. You're given a choice of which fighter to fly: a Spitfire or a Hurricane.

"The Spitfire is a beauty," your friend Tom says. "And fast."

239

"But the Hurricane is solid," you say. "If a German fighter blasts at you, the Hurricane can take a lot of bullets and keep on flying."

• To fly a Spitfire, turn to page 240.
• To fly a Hurricane, turn to page 255.

"I'll take speed over strength," you say. "After all, if the German planes can't catch you, they can't hurt you. I'll take the Spitfire."

By now it's the summer of 1940. While you're training, German troops are moving across western Europe. In June they seize France. Everyone is sure Great Britain will be Hitler's next target.

By August the Germans are sending hundreds of bombers to attack Britain. It's your mission to stop them. Joining you are fellow pilots from across the British Empire—New Zealand, Canada, Australia. Others are from countries the Nazis have defeated, such as Czechoslovakia and Poland. Your commander assigns you as Red Two, one of three planes in your section.

Thanks to the new invention of radar, you know that German planes are heading for major cities along the coast. You head in that direction and discover that the planes are German bombers called Heinkel 111s. These He 111 bombers lack much firepower. But you know they don't fly alone. Somewhere close by are German fighters, most likely Messerschmitt 109s.

An He 111 bombardier used a bombsight and maps to find targets.

Turn the page.

You want to attack the Me 109 fighters first, then come back for the bombers before they reach the coast. "Red Two, Red Two," you hear over your radio. "Bandits down below."

Now you see a group of six Me 109s. You and the other two planes swoop down to attack. In a moment your Spitfire is shaking from the force of all your machine guns firing at once.

Your bullets score a direct hit. Black smoke streams from one of the German planes. You turn to attack another Me 109. This time the enemy pilot fires first.

One explosive bullet rips into your cockpit, and tiny pieces of metal strike your arm. You grit your teeth but keep going. With a roll of your plane, you come up behind the Me 109. Another blast of your guns sends this one down too.

The other planes in your squadron have taken care of the rest of the fighters. Now you close in on an He 111. You take aim at one of its two engines. After a short blast of your guns, the bomber's engine begins to smoke. But maybe you should fire again, to make sure you've gotten it.

• To let the He 111 land, turn to page 253.

• To attack again, turn to page 254.

No matter the danger, you'll feel better being in your own plane. "Does anyone else know about the engine?" you ask Burt. He shakes his head no. "Good. Don't tell them."

As you slide the hood shut, Burt calls out, "If your engine cuts out, you might not get it back."

You wave, then head off down the runway. The Blitz, as this part of the Battle of Britain is called, has led to thousands of deaths. But you and the other British pilots have an advantage—radar. This new invention lets radio stations on the ground detect German planes when they take off. You and the other fighters know where the enemy is heading.

Down below you see a group of German fighter planes—Me 109s. The German fighter is just as fast as your Spitfire, and it carries better guns. It can also climb and dive faster than the Spitfire, but the Spitfire can turn quicker. You've had dogfights before with Me 109s and always survived. You begin to move down to attack one of the enemy planes.

You fly behind an Me 109 and begin to fire your machine guns. A direct hit! But as you watch that plane spiral down to the ground, two more Me 109s come toward you. You begin to dive, but your engine cuts out. The dive has cut off the flow of gas to your engine—one problem with the Spitfire. Normally the gas flows again, but not this time.

245

Turn the page.

You remember what Burt said, as the enemy bullets hit your plane. Your cockpit fills with smoke. Coughing and struggling to breathe, you release the hatch and jump into the sky. You pull the cord on your parachute and begin to catch your breath. But just when you think you're out of danger, you're stabbed with a blinding pain. Bullets from an Me 109 rip into you as you fall. You're dead before you hit the ground.

246

THE END
To follow another path, turn to page 229.
To read the conclusion, turn to page 319.

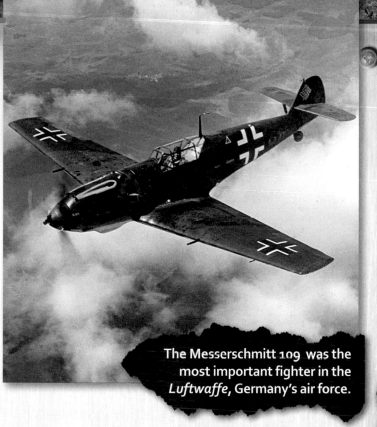

The Messerschmitt 109 was the most important fighter in the *Luftwaffe*, Germany's air force.

You radio Archie and tell him to look out for the approaching Me 109. You and the German plane are heading right for one another, nose to nose. The only difference is that his guns are working. He fires. More bullets rip into your Spitfire, but somehow they miss your engine and other important parts.

Turn the page.

At that last instant, you put the nose down and try to pass underneath the Me 109. But it's too late and you're too close. With the deafening crash of metal on metal, you collide with the Me 109.

The cockpit immediately fills with smoke. Flames begin to leap from the engine. You try to open the hood, but the metal holding it in place is too damaged. There's no way to parachute out.

You have only one hope: crash-land the Spitfire. The plane is already diving downward. You pull up on the stick and try to regain control. Through the smoke, you can tell you are flying over land. You aim for a flat area and hope for the best.

Your speed is down to about 100 miles per hour when you hit. You bounce around in the cockpit as the plane plows through wooden fence posts. At last the plane comes to a rest.

The hood, though, still won't open. Flames are pouring out of the engine. You reach for the crowbar all the Spitfires have and strike the glass with it. You squeeze out of the cockpit, cutting your arms and legs. As you stagger away, you look back to see the whole plane go up in flames.

You look up and see more Me 109s closing in on Archie. You watch with horror as his plane explodes from German gunfire. You're alive, but your friend is dead. You'll always regret that you couldn't save him.

249

THE END

To follow another path, turn to page 229.
To read the conclusion, turn to page 319.

It's too dangerous to help Archie. As you head back to base, you see a German Me 110 approach—another fighter. Its cannons are powerful, but your plane can turn sharper and faster in a dogfight.

The Me 110 comes barreling toward you, its cannons blazing. You dive and roll and use all your skills to dodge the shots. But some still find their mark, ripping into your plane and damaging your rudder.

You dive down, hoping the other pilot will think you're going to crash. The Me 110 flies off. Just in time, you pull back on the stick to come out of your dive and head back to base. As soon as you land, you plan to have a talk with the armorer who forgot to load the guns.

The next day you learn that Archie didn't make it. The news hits you like a punch to the stomach. You are sad to know he's gone. But you're also proud of him—you know he went down fighting.

RAF pilot gear included parachutes, harnesses, and warm sheepskin flying jackets.

THE END
To follow another path, turn to page 229.
To read the conclusion, turn to page 319.

The next day you talk to your sergeant. You tell him you're not sure you still want to be a pilot.

"Plenty of trainees wash out and don't get their wings," he says. "But you said you wanted to be part of the RAF. We'll see about getting you another job. We need navigators and radio operators."

The sergeant is right. You asked to join. You realize you'll just have to try your best through the rest of the training and do what you can to help fight the Germans.

252

THE END

To follow another path, turn to page 229.
To read the conclusion, turn to page 319.

You pull alongside the He 111 and try to flag the pilot. More smoke is pouring out, and you know he'll never reach his target. You point to the ground and mouth the words, "Go down! Land!" The German pilot sees you and nods. He understands that you will let him land rather than shoot him down.

You watch as he lands and a police car races up. The German crew will be taken as prisoners of war. As you fly over the men, the bomber pilot waves. You are enemies, but you still respect one another. You head back to base, knowing you will have more missions to fly before the day is done.

253

THE END

To follow another path, turn to page 229.
To read the conclusion, turn to page 319.

You circle up and over the He 111 to come at it from behind. You fire another round of bullets. These hit the other engine, and soon the German bomber is crashing below you.

"Got him!" you yell. But your celebration doesn't last long. Just as you're turning to look for another bomber, an Me 109 comes at you, blasting. You're hit! You have only seconds to prepare for your death as your Spitfire plummets to the ground in flames. You die on impact, just yards from the German bomber you shot down.

254

THE END
To follow another path, turn to page 229.
To read the conclusion, turn to page 319.

"I like the idea of surviving enemy fire," you say. You go with the Hurricane.

One rainy day in August, you head out on a mission. You spy German bombers called Dornier 17s. With the Do 17s is a group of fighters. Your plane is in the first group of Hurricanes closing in for the attack.

Before you can fire your guns, tracers from the Me 109s streak past you. Your plane's been hit! You have only a few seconds to act before flames fill the cockpit.

Turn the page.

Your pants catch fire as you release the hood of the plane to parachute out. Immediately you feel the searing heat reach your skin. In a panic, you leap. The rushing air puts out the flames on your clothing. You sigh in relief as your parachute brings you safely to the ground.

When you land, local men with shotguns are waiting for you. "Don't shoot!" you scream. "I'm British!" You pull your ID card out of your charred pants. As you are driven to the base, you realize how badly your legs are burned. But the wounds are worth it, if you can help defeat the Nazis.

256

THE END
To follow another path, turn to page 229.
To read the conclusion, turn to page 319.

Thousands of WWII airmen became members of the "Caterpillar Club" when their lives were saved by parachutes. The club is named for the silkworm because the parachutes were made from their silk.

An American bomber crew prepared for a mission.

CHAPTER 3

FLYING IN THE PACIFIC

You were still in high school when the Japanese bombed Pearl Harbor in 1941. You wanted to fight, but you were too young. Now it's 1944. You're done with school and ready to do your part. You want to become a pilot. You and your friend Jimmy plan to enlist together.

"Should we join the Navy or the Army?" Jimmy asks.

"Those Navy fighter pilots have the Hellcat," you say. "I'd love to fly one of those. It can do almost 400 miles per hour!" You know that Navy pilots flying Hellcats have been scoring many kills against the Zero, the top Japanese fighter.

259

Turn the page.

"But the Army Air Force has some great planes too," Jimmy says. "The P-51 Mustang is even faster than the Hellcat. You could fly along to protect those big bombers that are really doing damage to Germany. Or maybe fly a bomber yourself, and attack some Japanese ships."

• To join the Navy, go to page 261.

• To join the Army Air Force, turn to page 268.

"I've always wanted to go to sea," you say. "And I've always wanted to fly. I think being a Navy pilot is the best bet for me."

Your training starts at a naval air station. From there the Navy sends you to a training school run by civilians to see if you can handle a small aircraft. After some lessons you fly a Piper Cub, a two-seat trainer. The Cub is tiny and slow compared to the Hellcats you hope to fly. But in it you convince the Navy you have the skills needed to be a pilot.

You move on to the University of Iowa, where the Navy has a preflight training school. Over several months, you learn how to operate a radio and navigate a plane.

Turn the page.

Your next stop is a flight training school in Florida. After months of hard work, you earn your wings—you are a Navy pilot. Now you will complete your training on the plane you'll fly in combat. All along you've been thinking about flying the Hellcat fighter. But now you realize how important torpedo bombers are too.

One of the bombers Navy pilots fly in the Pacific is the Avenger. The Avenger can take out enemy ships, and its machine guns are powerful enough to shoot down Japanese planes.

• *To fly the Avenger torpedo bomber, go to page 263.*

• *To fly the Hellcat fighter, turn to page 266.*

The USS *San Jacinto* carried 45 aircraft and more than 1,500 men.

You pick the Avenger. It has a radioman and a gunner, and you like the idea of flying with a crew.

Early in 1945 you are assigned to the aircraft carrier *San Jacinto*. Each day you practice taking off and landing on a moving ship.

263

Turn the page.

In February you're assigned your first combat flight. Your ship is part of a major assault on the Japanese island of Iwo Jima. You take off with your usual crew. Buddy is the radioman, and Ted is the gunner. You are separated from your crew by a metal plate, so you communicate by radio.

You carry bombs as you head for the island. As you approach, black smoke from Japanese anti-aircraft guns fills the air. Even with the smoke, you manage to find your target and drop your 500-pound bombs.

"I think we got them!" you say, squinting to see through the smoke below. But as you circle the Avenger to head back to the ship, anti-aircraft fire rips into the plane. Your cockpit fills with smoke. Gasping for air, you radio to the crew, "We've been hit! Get ready to jump!"

Neither Buddy nor Ted radios back. What if they've been injured? Should you leave the plane without checking?

265

• To parachute out, turn to page 276.

• To check on your crew, turn to page 277.

After training you're assigned to a new aircraft carrier, the USS *Randolph*. In January 1945 it sails out of San Francisco for Ulithi, an island thousands of miles away in the Pacific.

As you sail you practice an aerial move called the Thach Weave. It helps American pilots avoid getting shot down by the best Japanese fighter plane, the Zero.

A pilot named Frank works with you on the Thach Weave. He's an "ace," which means that he's shot down at least five enemy planes. "We fly side by side," Frank explains, "but spaced apart. If a Zero comes up on our tail, we start to crisscross each other. The Zero will pick one of us to follow—and the other one of us will have a clear shot at him."

When the *Randolph* reaches Ulithi, you receive your orders. You and other fighter pilots will fly with bombers sent to attack Japan.

The Mitsubishi A6M Zero, a long-range fighter used by the Japanese, had a flying range of more than 1,200 miles.

Turn to page 274.

Jimmy is right—the Army has great planes too. You go with him to an Army recruiting office. After taking tests and a physical exam, you get the good word—you've both made it. But the road to actually flying is a long one. And you receive some bad news. At 6 feet, you're too tall for the 5-foot 8-inch height limit to fly the Mustang fighter. Maybe being a bomber pilot won't be so bad.

You and Jimmy take a train to the Army Air Force base in Santa Ana, California. At the base you go through more training and testing. The tests are hard, but both of you make it.

Then you head to another California base for flight training. The training is intense. About 25 percent of the cadets drop out of the program.

After months of hard work, you and Jimmy earn your wings. Now you'll go for your final training on the planes you'll fly in combat. You'll be flying one of the bombers, either a B-24 or B-25.

The B-24 has four engines, so it can take a lot of engine damage and keep flying. But that plane is strictly a high-altitude bomber, and it requires an oxygen mask. The B-25 can go on various missions, including hunting enemy submarines and scouting out enemy activity.

269

• To fly a B-24, turn to page 270.

• To fly a B-25, turn to page 282.

You finish your final training on a B-24. Then your squadron heads to a base in India, which is a British colony. From there your squadron begins to carry out bombing missions. You'll be attacking Japanese bases in Burma, a country between India and China.

Unlike most bombers, you fly without fighter planes to protect you. The route is too far for the fighters. They can't carry enough fuel. But your B-24 has 10 machine guns positioned around the plane. Along with your gunners, your crew includes a co-pilot, a navigator, a radio operator, and a bombardier.

One night your plane takes off, heading for railways the Japanese use to move supplies. You reach the target and drop your bombs. But on the way back, several Japanese fighters approach.

You hear tracers streak past the plane. These bullets have chemicals inside that create a trail of smoke. The whistling sound is followed by the loud rat-a-tat of your guns firing back. Then you hear a cry—Roy, a gunner, has been hit by enemy bullets.

"We've got a bandit right on our tail," your co-pilot, Bill, says.

Your B-24 is too slow to outrun the Zero. You think about how to shake him—if you can.

"Look at those mountains ahead," Joe, the navigator, calls. "I can guide you down low enough so we might be able to get that Zero to crash into them."

"But if we go too low, we could crash too," Bill says.

271

• To fly toward the mountain, turn to page 272.

• To turn away from the mountain, turn to page 285.

You begin to lower the B-24, to get closer to the approaching mountain. The Zero has to stay about 400 feet beneath you to get into the best position to attack. You're hoping that in the darkness he can't see the mountain ahead of you. You follow the navigator's directions as he guides you close to the mountainside. Closer, closer—and you zoom over the rocky peak. A second later you glance back and see a huge ball of fire fill the night sky.

"It worked!" Bill says. Over the radio you hear the crew cheering. You head back to base while the bombardier takes care of Roy. He's going to be all right, and you and your crew have survived another mission.

The next day a general approaches you. He heard about your bravery the night before. "We need good pilots like you in other parts of Asia," he says. "We have a secret mission you might want to consider. Or, if you're open for learning something new, you can fly a B-25 in the Philippines."

• *To go to the Philippines, turn to page 282.*

• *To accept the secret mission, turn to page 287.*

You climb into your cockpit. Frank walks by and leans in before getting into his plane. "You're my wingman," he says. You nod and give him the thumbs up.

You and your squadron head for Tokyo. As you near the target, you see Zeroes approaching you. They want to lure the Hellcats away from the bombers, so other Zeroes can attack the bombers. But everyone in your squadron follows orders and stays with the Avengers. Closer to the target, though, dozens more Zeroes are waiting.

You fly toward the Zeroes and right away are surrounded. You twist and turn to avoid one Zero and find yourself on the tail of another. With a burst from your machine guns, one Zero goes down.

To the left you see a Zero closing in on Frank's plane. But in the other direction, a pack of Zeroes is heading for several Avengers. No other fighters are around to protect the bombers. Do you help your friend, or help the bombers carry out their mission?

Crewmen used catapults to launch aircraft, including Hellcats, into flight.

• To help Frank, turn to page 278.

• To help the Avengers, turn to page 279.

You hate to leave your crew, but your instincts tell you to save yourself. You get your parachute ready and open the cockpit. Now you see the wings are on fire. "I hope Buddy and Ted get out OK," you think, as you leap from the burning plane. After a few seconds, you pull the cord that opens the parachute. There's no sign of your crew.

You make a hard landing into the Pacific Ocean. Your life vest keeps you on the surface as you fumble to open your raft. Now, all you can do is hope a U.S. ship rescues you soon. As you drift in the sea, you think about Buddy and Ted, knowing they must have been killed. You'll always wonder if you could have saved them.

THE END

To follow another path, turn to page 229.
To read the conclusion, turn to page 319.

276

You radio Ted and Buddy again. This time you hear a faint sound—Buddy's voice. "I've been hit," he says. "Ted too. We can't jump, but you go."

"Not a chance, Buddy," you say. "Prepare for a water landing." You bring the Avenger down low toward the ocean, cutting the speed. With a thud the plane lands in the water. "Can you get out?" you radio to Buddy.

"I think so, but we might need some help."

But then you see a Japanese ship approaching. Sailors on deck are pointing guns at you. You've survived the crash, but now all three of you are about to become prisoners of war.

THE END
To follow another path, turn to page 229.
To read the conclusion, turn to page 319.

You open up the throttle all the way and speed toward the Zero that's attacking Frank. He radios to you, "Get in position so we can weave!"

As the Zero tries to get behind Frank, you start the Thach Weave. After a few crosses, you have the Zero right in front of you. You fire ahead of the plane, to the spot where you expect it to be in a split second. Your bullets hit their target. The Zero bursts into flames.

You're close enough now to see Frank in his cockpit. "Pretty soon you'll be an ace like me," he radios.

The bombers have hit their targets. It's time to head back to the *Randolph*. Maybe you'll become an ace on your next mission.

THE END

To follow another path, turn to page 229.
To read the conclusion, turn to page 319.

You're sure that Frank will be OK. The Avengers need you more. You see them firing their guns, trying to shoot down the much faster and sharper-turning Zeroes attacking them.

You close in on the nearest Zero, so your machine guns will be in range. Your bullets blast into the engine, sending the plane down. Now Frank and several other Hellcats have joined you in defending the Avengers. Together you shoot down two more enemy planes. The rest fly off before you can get them. You stick with the Avengers as they bomb their targets, and then you all return to the *Randolph*.

279

Turn the page.

For several weeks you don't fly any missions. The *Randolph* anchors at Ulithi. On the night of March 11, the pilots and sailors watch a movie called *A Song to Remember* on the hangar deck. Just as the movie is ending, you hear the noise of a single plane approaching the ship. Through the darkness you can't tell what it is, but you have a bad feeling.

It's a kamikaze! And it's coming straight for the ship with the aim to kill as many as possible.

The Japanese know they are losing the war in the Pacific. They've begun using kamikazes to attack U.S. ships. These bomb-loaded planes fly into their targets, exploding on impact. The Japanese pilots know they will die as they try to carry out their mission.

The USS *Randolph* docked alongside a repair ship after it was damaged by a kamikaze.

Within seconds it hits. A fiery explosion shakes the ship, and a piece of metal tears into your leg. You scream as you collapse on the deck. Through the smoke you see Frank crumpled nearby, unmoving. You call out to him to see if he's alive. As you wait for an answer that never comes, you slowly close your eyes for the last time.

281

THE END

To follow another path, turn to page 229.
To read the conclusion, turn to page 319.

You finish your final training with a B-25. Then your squadron ships out to a small island in the Pacific Ocean called Morotai, close to the Philippines. For your first mission, your target is the Philippine island of Mindanao, where the Japanese have an airfield. You'll fly your B-25 at low altitude and use powerful machine guns to fire at the Japanese on the ground. Then you'll drop your bombs.

As you drop down just above the treetops, Japanese anti-aircraft guns fire up at you. But their aim is bad, and they miss. Other planes in your squadron have dropped their bombs.

"They scored some direct hits," your co-pilot, Smitty, says.

"Yeah," you say, "but the smoke is so thick I can barely see the target."

You fire the B-25's machine guns as you prepare to release your bombs. With the push of a button, a ton of bombs shoot out of the plane. You pull up to begin the flight back to Morotai.

B-25s headed toward islands in the Pacific Ocean to bomb Japanese air bases.

Turn the page.

"We got 'em hard!" your radioman says, seeing that your bombs have hit the target. But your flight back might not be an easy one. Japanese Zeroes are approaching. You can't outfly them—they're faster than you. You shoot at a Zero just as he fires his cannon at you. Your B-25 takes a direct hit to the cockpit.

You feel pain in your chest and look down and see blood. "I'm hit!" you say. You feel weak. You try to warn your crew—"Get out while you ..." But you never finish the sentence. The last thing you see is the nose of your plane as it spirals into the ocean below.

284

THE END
To follow another path, turn to page 229.
To read the conclusion, turn to page 319.

"It's too risky to fly that low," you say. You begin to turn and see two more Zeroes approaching in the faint moonlight. You feel your body tense. The enemy bullets hit the plane, making a noise like hammering metal. Your gunners fire and score several direct hits. The men cheer as one Zero explodes. Another goes down in a fiery streak.

"Just one left," Bill says. "And he's already taken some hits." Still, the Zero has enough power to fire again. An explosion tells you he's scored a hit. "Number two engine is out," Bill says. "But that Zero is nowhere in sight."

"How's Roy?" you radio to the back of the plane.

"We stopped the bleeding," the bombardier says. "He'll be OK."

Turn the page.

"Then let's get home," you say, heading back toward the base. In a few minutes, though, you feel a shudder. You've been hit again. Another engine! "Good thing we have two more," Joe says. "And I've heard some B-24s have even made it back with just one engine."

"I don't want to push our luck," you say. You feel the plane start to lose altitude. "Throw out anything we don't need," you order. You hate to lose the valuable equipment, but you have to. The lighter you are, the easier it is to fly with only two engines. The crew tosses out guns and heavy equipment. Finally, you see the lights of the air base ahead of you. You've made it back in one piece—this time.

THE END
To follow another path, turn to page 229.
To read the conclusion, turn to page 319.

For your new mission, you learn to fly a B-29, the newest Air Force bomber. Unlike your old B-24, the guns are fired by remote control. Also, the plane is pressurized, so you won't need to wear an oxygen mask.

After your training you and your flight group head to a huge air base on Tinian, a Pacific island. From there your B-29 can easily reach targets in Japan. In the summer of 1945, you finally learn what the secret mission is all about.

An officer explains it to your group: "Our scientists have developed a new weapon—the atomic bomb. Just one of these bombs can destroy large parts of a city. With this bomb we can end the war—and save the lives of many American soldiers."

Turn the page.

When the final orders come, you aren't assigned to fly the *Enola Gay*, the B-29 that will carry the bomb. Instead, you're the co-pilot of another plane, the *Great Artiste*. It will carry scientists who will measure the destructive force of the bomb.

The B-29 *Enola Gay* dropped the world's first atomic bomb August 6, 1945.

On August 6 the planes take off from Tinian. Over the Japanese city of Hiroshima, the *Enola Gay* releases the atomic bomb. It drifts down on a parachute, so both planes will have time to get away before the massive explosion. In 43 seconds the explosion comes. A moment later you feel a wave of energy bounce against your plane. The bomb has worked!

You and the rest of the crew look back and see a huge cloud of thick white smoke rising tens of thousands of feet into the air. You hope the officers are right—that dropping this bomb will finally end the war.

THE END
To follow another path, turn to page 229.
To read the conclusion, turn to page 319.

Tuskegee Airman Edward Gleed
flew a P-51 Mustang in the
332nd Fighter Group.

CHAPTER 4

THE TUSKEGEE AIRMEN

It's 1943, and you have just finished high school in Boston. The United States is heavily involved in World War II, and you want to help fight. You go to a recruiting office and tell the sergeant, "I want to fly for the Army Air Force."

"What are you talking about?" the sergeant says harshly. "The Army doesn't let Negroes fly planes."

"Yes, sir, it does," you say quietly, trying not to anger the sergeant. You've grown up surrounded by whites. You know some of them are racist. "The Army began accepting Negro cadets in 1941. There's a separate airfield to train them down in Alabama."

291

Turn the page.

"Never heard of it," the sergeant says. "Look, if you want to join the Army, maybe you can be a cook."

You walk out of the office. You go to another recruiting station. Then another. None of the sergeants say they have heard of Tuskegee Institute, where black pilots are already training. Finally, you find a station where the sergeant will listen to you. He tells you to report to Fort Devens, which is near Boston. You smile.

Everything goes well at Fort Devens. Next you need to decide what kind of plane you want to fly. You like the fighters because they're fast and make you think quickly. But you also like the idea of working with a team, as you would in a bomber.

- To train as a fighter pilot, go to page 293.
- To train as a bomber pilot, turn to page 298.

292

You decide to become a fighter pilot—or at least find out if you're good enough.

Within a week you're boarding a train to go to your basic training at Keesler Air Force Base in Biloxi, Mississippi. In Washington, D.C., you change trains and take a seat. A police officer comes up to you. "You can't sit here," he says. "Come with me." The officer leads you to a dirty, noisy seat near the coal, which powers the steam engine.

Trains and public buildings are segregated in the South. Blacks and whites don't sit together, and blacks are always treated worse. You feel anger rising inside you. You want to help your country. But the country's laws treat you unfairly. You wonder when blacks will get equal rights.

Turn the page.

After your training in Mississippi, you go to Tuskegee, Alabama. Later, all the pilots who train there will be called Tuskegee Airmen. One trainer has already flown dozens of combat missions with the Airmen. "We helped sink a German warship once," he tells you. "But mostly we protect the bombers from the German fighters."

You practice in many types of planes. One of them is the T-6, which has two seats—one for the student and one for the trainer. Captain Carl Simmons asks who wants to go on a training flight. You like flying with him because you learn a lot. But you see that Leon, another cadet you know, is eager to go. He doesn't have much experience yet. Maybe you should let Leon have a chance.

• To let the other cadet fly, go to page 295.

• To go on the training flight, turn to page 311.

While escorting U.S. bombers over Europe, the Tuskegee Airmen shot down more than 100 German planes.

"You go ahead," you tell Leon. "I'll get another chance to go with the captain."

Over the next few weeks, you complete your training at Tuskegee. Your next stop is a U.S. air base in Italy. You are a member of the new 301st Fighter Squadron, part of the 332nd Fighter Group. You'll be flying one of the best fighters in the sky—the P-51 Mustang.

Turn the page.

All the planes in the group have red paint on their tails. The American bomber pilots call the Airmen "Red Tail Angels." You and the other Tuskegee pilots have won the respect of the white pilots. You're known for keeping the bombers safe.

As the months go by, you fly many missions. One day you see a different kind of German plane swooping down from the clouds above. You realize right away that it's the new plane other pilots have talked about. The Me 262 is the world's first fighter plane with a jet engine. It flies faster than anything else in the skies.

This one is closing in on you. Your Mustang can't outfly it, but you can turn more quickly.

You try to get into the best position to fire. Another Mustang flies nearby while the Me 262 turns, hoping to fire its cannons at you. Before the pilot can fire, you dive down. The bullets from his guns whistle past you.

You glance over and see an Me 109 approaching. It's not a jet plane, but it's still fast. Before you can get out of the way, its guns fire. You hear some of the bullets tear into the side of your plane.

"I'm hit," you radio to base. "Not sure how bad." Your plane is starting to lose oil. You should probably head back to base. But you don't want to go back without taking out that jet plane.

297

• To go after the Me 262, turn to page 305.

• To head back toward the base, turn to page 313.

In a few days, you take a train to Biloxi, Mississippi. At Keesler Air Base, you take more tests and go through basic training. Along with the flight training, you take college classes. The work is hard—much harder than high school. And the physical training is much tougher than anything you've ever done in gym. You tell James, another cadet, "I'm not sure I can make it as a pilot."

"They make it even harder for us Negroes," he says. "Some whites in the military want us to fail—just because we're black."

One day Sergeant Harvey Jones, a white airman you don't like, asks for a volunteer. "I want one of you to fly the China Clipper tomorrow morning," he says. "Who wants to do it?"

You and the other cadets look at each other. None of you have ever heard of the China Clipper. Maybe it's a new plane. It would be great to fly something new. But then you remember what another cadet once told you—never volunteer for anything in the Army. You never know what you're in for.

• *To volunteer, turn to page 300.*

• *To keep quiet, turn to page 303.*

You decide to volunteer. "Excellent," Sergeant Jones says. "I'll see you tomorrow at 0300 hours." Three o'clock in the morning! No one flies planes that early.

At 3 a.m. Jones leads you to the kitchen. He points at the dishwasher and says, "This is the China Clipper. Enjoy yourself, cadet." You see stacks of dishes all around. Maybe Jones would have tried to trick a white cadet too. But you feel that he enjoyed it more because you're black.

Now you're really not sure you want to be here at Tuskegee. The other cadets seem to know more than you, and you can't stand the racism. And maybe you're not a good enough pilot.

You find out when you go out for a check ride later that day—the flight that shows your skills. A white officer, Major Wallace Bendall, flies with you. You fly the plane through loops, rolls, and dives. But you can tell the test is not going well—the moves are not as sharp as they should be. You have a feeling you're going to wash out.

Airmen lined up for inspection at Randolph Air Force Base.

Turn the page.

The next day you get the news you were expecting. "I'm afraid you don't have what it takes to be a pilot," Major Bendall says. "But a bomber needs other crewmembers. You could be a gunner or a navigator."

You know you can still help your country on a bomber crew. But maybe you should leave the Army Air Force altogether, to escape the racism.

• To become a bomber crew member, turn to page 308.

• To consider leaving the Army Air Force, turn to page 310.

James steps forward. You're glad you didn't volunteer, because you later learn that the China Clipper is a nickname for a dishwasher. James had to get up at 3 a.m. to wash dishes!

When your training is finished at Tuskegee, you earn your wings. You transfer to Freeman Field in Indiana. You're assigned to a squadron that is part of the 477th Bombardment Group. Now you have more training on the plane you will fly in combat—the B-25 bomber.

You've earned the rank of second lieutenant, making you an officer. In the military, officers have their own clubs where they can relax when they're not on duty. But you learn that black officers don't have equal rights. They can't use the club that white officers use.

Turn the page.

A group of black officers meets to discuss what is happening. "This is crazy," Captain Coleman Young says. "White bomber groups get sent overseas a lot faster than we do. It's like they don't want us to fight."

"Yeah," Lieutenant Harold Smith says. "And they don't face the unfair treatment we do here at home."

"We have to do something about this," Young says. "We should go into that white officers' club and demand our rights."

304

Turn to page 315.

You see the other Mustangs from your group approaching. More German planes have arrived too, and dogfights start all over the skies. You keep your eye on that first Me 262—that's the one you want. You circle around him and fire your guns. It's a direct hit! The plane tumbles to the ground.

"That's a kill," another pilot radios. "Nice shooting."

You glance down at the oil gauge. It's fallen quickly since you were hit. Just then, bullets pour into the tail of your plane. A German has come up from behind. Black smoke billows into the cockpit, choking you. Your plane is going down, and you have only one choice now—jump.

Turn the page.

To your surprise, the German fighters don't fire at you as you parachute to the ground. But as you land, you see German soldiers running toward you with guns. They take you to a prisoner of war camp called Stalag Luft III.

A German officer questions you in English. You give him the only information a prisoner is supposed to give—name, rank, and serial number.

In the camp are several thousand British and American airmen. Most of them are white. You wonder how the Americans will treat you. An American from one barracks comes over to you and shakes your hand. "I'm Airman Mike Thompson," he says in a southern drawl. "We want you to stay with us."

"OK," you say. Inside the barracks you find out why Mike wanted you.

Prisoners of war were counted during roll call twice a day at Stalag Luft III.

"The Germans sometimes sneak in one of their own men who speaks good English," he says. "They're planting spies. The Germans want to know if we're planning an escape." Mike smiles. "But I've never seen a black German pilot before, so I figured you must be one of us."

You don't know what's in store for you, but at least you're among fellow Allied airmen.

THE END

To follow another path, turn to page 229.
To read the conclusion, turn to page 319.

The major arranges for you to take some
tests, to see what you could do on a bomber crew.
You score well on the math skills needed to be a
bombardier, so you head for training at Midland
Army Air Base in Texas. You work with one of
the first secret weapons of the war, the Norden
bombsight. The device takes information you
enter into it and decides the exact moment when
the bombs should be released.

When your training is done, you wait for your
orders to go into combat and prove your skills.
But the Army is dragging its feet, just like it did
with black fighter pilots, and you don't get the
chance. The black bomber pilots are never sent
into combat before the end of the war.

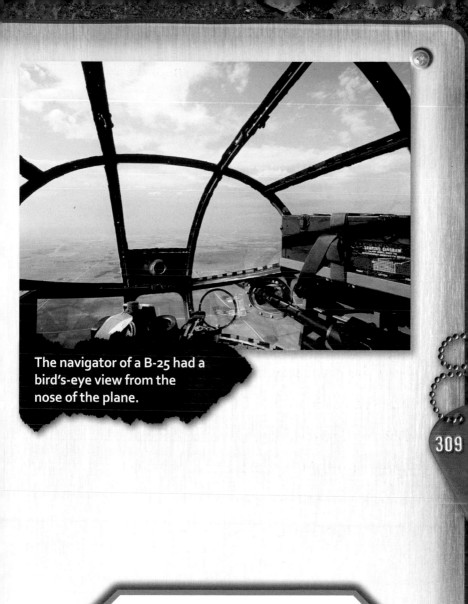

The navigator of a B-25 had a bird's-eye view from the nose of the plane.

THE END

To follow another path, turn to page 229.
To read the conclusion, turn to page 319.

"You can leave the Air Force for another Army unit, if that's what you want," the major says. "But you might not like the assignment you end up with instead."

You wonder where you'll be assigned. You know that just a few Army units are integrated—blacks and whites serving together. But in many cases, the blacks get the jobs that don't take much skill. They cook food or drive trucks. But your time at Tuskegee has shown you that you're pretty smart. You'll show the Army what you can do to fight—even if it won't be from the cockpit.

310

THE END

To follow another path, turn to page 229.
To read the conclusion, turn to page 319.

"I need all the hours I can get up in the air," you say as you step forward.

"I like your attitude," Captain Simmons says with a smile. "Let's go."

You began your training in an old biplane. The T-6 you're flying today is more like the fighters used in combat. It's not as fast as a Mustang, but it can do the same kinds of moves in the air. You climb inside the cockpit behind the captain. Before you know it, you're airborne with Simmons at the controls.

"I want to show you a new move," he says. "We're going to do an inverted roll." You know what's coming—the plane will roll on its side, so for a split second you'll be flying upside down.

Turn the page.

You brace yourself for the roll. But suddenly you feel yourself falling from your seat—your seatbelt has snapped! You grab at anything you can to stay in the plane. "Captain!" you yell.

You hold on, but Captain Simmons loses control of the plane. You're filled with terror. You see the ground zooming closer through the windshield of the T-6 as it hurtles downward. You die before you ever see battle.

312

THE END

To follow another path, turn to page 229.
To read the conclusion, turn to page 319.

"I'm losing oil," you radio. "I'm turning back." You watch the oil gauge move lower and lower. You keep flying, looking for a field to land in—you hope not one on German soil. You want to reach Yugoslavia. Many people there are fighting the Germans. The partisans help Allied pilots when they can.

You see an open space up ahead and start to bring the Mustang down. You go in on the plane's belly, since it's too dangerous to land on your wheels. You keep your speed at about 120 miles per hour until you're just about to hit the ground. The plane lands with a thud and bounces a few times before sliding to a stop.

Turn the page.

A kind farmer, whose field you've landed in, helps you to his house. Because of his warm welcome you realize that he's Yugoslavian, though you can't understand what he's saying.

You don't know how long it will take you to get back to base. But at least for the moment you're alive and safe.

314

THE END
To follow another path, turn to page 229.
To read the conclusion, turn to page 319.

"I'll go with you into the club," you say. Young smiles and draws up a plan. On the first night several groups of officers will go into the club. The next night another group will go. You volunteer for the second group.

The first night does not go well. The black officers are arrested and forced to stay in the barracks. The next night you feel a little nervous as you and several other African-American officers enter the club. A white major is waiting for you. "You know you're not allowed in this club," he says.

You take a deep breath and find the courage to speak. "Under Army and U.S. government rules, we should be allowed in." He places you under arrest.

Turn the page.

The next day Colonel Robert Selway closes the club. He writes a statement outlining the policy of separate clubs for white and black officers. He wants all the officers to sign the statement to show they accept it. You are called into a room where a white officer asks you to sign. You refuse.

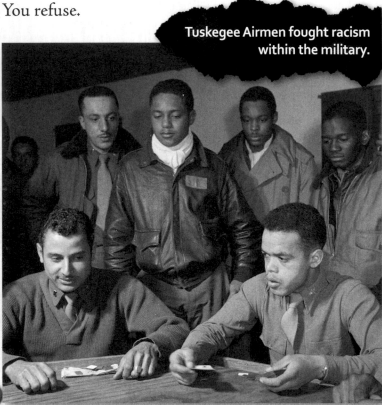

Tuskegee Airmen fought racism within the military.

You soon learn that 101 black officers refused to sign Selway's policy. If you are found guilty of disobeying an order, you could go to prison and lose your rank, or worse. Soon all of you are relocated to Godman Field in Kentucky.

After a few days, on April 23, 1945, you receive good news. The top Army general, George C. Marshall, has ordered you all released. And from now on, the 477th will have a black commanding officer. But by the time this happens, the war is almost over. You will never fly a bomber in combat. But at least you know you stood up for what was right.

317

THE END
To follow another path, turn to page 229.
To read the conclusion, turn to page 319.

A British Avenger torpedo bomber flew over the HMS *Indomitable* aircraft carrier during a bombing exercise.

CHAPTER 5

BRAVERY IN THE AIR

Even before World War II began, the world's leading nations saw that planes would play a huge role in warfare. The Americans and the British focused on building bombers that could fly long distances and carry heavy loads of bombs. The Germans built planes that could help their soldiers on the battlefield.

When the United States entered the war, much of its air power was based at sea on aircraft carriers. The Japanese and U.S. navies fought the world's first sea battles in which the enemy ships could not see each other. Almost all the fighting took place between carrier-based planes.

During the war the countries tried to improve their planes when they could. The United States introduced faster fighters, such as the Hellcat and the Mustang. German pilots flew the world's first jet plane, called the Swallow (Me 262).

A new U.S. bomber, the B-29, dropped bombs that caused deadly fires in Japanese cities. B-29s also dropped the world's first atomic bombs, killing or wounding several hundred thousand people. Those bombs helped end the war with Japan.

RAF flyers returned home after a successful mission.

321

Just as important as the planes used were the pilots who flew them. They carried out many kinds of missions while facing enemy fire from land and from other planes. They learned how to fire their guns, drop bombs and torpedoes, and avoid enemy planes. They parachuted out if their planes got hit. And at times pilots and their crews crash-landed. At sea, they risked drowning. They also faced capture by the enemy and becoming prisoners of war.

The pilots of World War II showed great bravery and skill as they carried out their missions. And the pilots known as the Tuskegee Airmen battled racism in their struggle to help defend their country. The U.S. military ended segregation in 1948, so anyone with the skills can now be a pilot.

Today's military pilots fly faster planes with better technology. But like the pilots of World War II, they rely on courage and talent to survive the dangers of war.

TIMELINE

1903—The first airplane flight takes place.

1914—World War I starts.

1918—World War I ends, and Germany is soon forced to give up most of its military.

1933—Adolf Hitler comes to power in Germany and begins secretly building a new air force.

1939—On **September 1** German troops invade Poland, starting World War II.

1940—Germany takes control of France in **June** after invading other western European nations.

In **August** German planes begin a major attack on Great Britain, known as the Battle of Britain.

1941—On **December 7** Japanese planes attack Pearl Harbor, Hawaii, bringing the United States into World War II.

1942—The first Tuskegee Airmen receive their wings and become military pilots.

The Battle of the Coral Sea marks the first time enemy naval ships battle each other without seeing each other; planes based on aircraft carriers do the fighting.

1944—German pilots fly the world's first jet-powered airplane.

In **July** Tuskegee Airmen fly P-51 Mustang fighters for the first time.

On **March 11 a** kamikaze damages the USS *Randolph*, killing 25 crewmen.

1945—In **April** members of the 477th Bombardment Group, made up of Tuskegee Airmen, protest segregation at Freeman Field, Indiana.

World War II ends in Europe on **May 8**, V-E (Victory in Europe) Day.

On **August 6** a B-29 bomber called the *Enola Gay* drops the world's first atomic bomb on Hiroshima; another atomic bomb is dropped on Nagasaki three days later.

World War II ends in Asia on **August 14**.

1948—President Harry Truman ends segregation in the military.

OTHER PATHS
TO EXPLORE

In this book you've seen how the events of the past look different from three points of view. Perspectives on history are as varied as the people who lived it. Seeing history from many points of view is an important part of understanding it.

Here are ideas for other World War II points of view to explore:

+ You are a female pilot flying planes for the RAF or the U.S. Army Air Force. You take planes where they are needed and help pilots and anti-aircraft gunners train. In Great Britain you take the planes to the front lines. How would you feel if male pilots said women shouldn't be allowed to fly?

+ You are a German bomber pilot setting off for England during the Blitz. You know your target is a city filled with civilians—including many women and children. How do you feel about having to attack them?

+ More than 40,000 members of the Army Air Force were captured by the enemy during World War II, usually after being shot down. These prisoners of war often suffered harsh treatment. What would it have been like to be a POW held by the Germans or Japanese?

AUTHOR
BIOGRAPHIES

Michael Burgan

Michael Burgan has written numerous books for children and young adults. Many of his books have focused on U.S. history, geography, and the lives of world leaders. Michael has won several awards for his writing, and his graphic novel version of the classic tale *Frankenstein* (Stone Arch Books) was a *Junior Library Guild* selection.

Steven Otfinoski

Steven Otfinoski has written more than 150 books for young readers. Three of his nonfiction books have been chosen Books for the Teen Age by the New York Public Library. Steve is also a playwright and has his own theater company that brings one-person plays about American history to schools.

Elizabeth Raum

Elizabeth Raum has written many nonfiction books for children. She has also written picture books and books for adults. Two of her Capstone You Choose books, *Orphan Trains* (2011) and *Can You Survive Storm Chasing?* (2012), are Junior Library Guild selections.